W9-BNY-011

30Jan'80

## 1980s Project Studies/Council on Foreign Relations

DIVERSITY AND DEVELOPMENT IN SOUTHEAST ASIA:

The Coming Decade

*Studies by Guy J. Pauker, Frank H. Golay, and Cynthia H. Enloe*

NUCLEAR WEAPONS AND WORLD POLITICS:

Alternatives for the Future

*Studies by David C. Gompert, Michael Mandelbaum, Richard L. Garwin, and John H. Barton*

CHINA'S FUTURE:

Foreign Policy and Economic Development in the Post-Mao Era

*Studies by Allen S. Whiting and Robert F. Dernberger*

ALTERNATIVES TO MONETARY DISORDER

*Studies by Fred Hirsch and Michael W. Doyle and by Edward L. Morse*

NUCLEAR PROLIFERATION:

Motivations, Capabilities, and Strategies for Control

*Studies by Ted Greenwood and by Harold A. Feiveson and Theodore B. Taylor*

INTERNATIONAL DISASTER RELIEF:

Toward a Responsive System

*Stephen Green*


**STUDIES FORTHCOMING**


The 1980s Project will comprise about 30 volumes. Most will contain independent but related studies concerning issues of potentially great importance in the next decade and beyond, such as resource management, human rights, population studies, and relations between the developing and developed societies, among many others. Additionally, a number of volumes will be devoted to particular regions of the world, concentrating especially on political and economic development trends outside the industrialized West.

# Africa
# in the 1980s

## A CONTINENT IN CRISIS

*COLIN LEGUM*

*I. WILLIAM ZARTMAN*

*STEVEN LANGDON and LYNN K. MYTELKA*

Introduction by Catherine Gwin

*1980s PROJECT/COUNCIL ON FOREIGN RELATIONS*

McGRAW-HILL BOOK COMPANY

New York   St. Louis   San Francisco
Auckland   Bogotá   Düsseldorf   Johannesburg   London   Madrid
Mexico   Montreal   New Delhi   Panama   Paris   São Paulo
Singapore   Sydney   Tokyo   Toronto

Wingate College Library

DT
30
A347

Copyright © 1979 by the Council on Foreign Relations, Inc. All rights reserved. Printed in the United States of America. No part of this publication may be reproduced, stored in a retrieval system, or transmitted, in any form or by any means, electronic, mechanical, photocopying, recording, or otherwise, without the prior written permission of the publisher.

The Council on Foreign Relations, Inc., is a nonprofit and nonpartisan organization devoted to promoting improved understanding of international affairs through the free exchange of ideas. Its membership of about 1,700 persons throughout the United States is made up of individuals with special interest and experience in international affairs. The Council has no affiliation with and receives no funding from the United States government.

The Council publishes the journal *Foreign Affairs* and, from time to time, books and monographs that in the judgment of the Council's Committee on Studies are responsible treatments of significant international topics worthy of presentation to the public. The 1980s Project is a research effort of the Council; as such, 1980s Project Studies have been similarly reviewed through procedures of the Committee on Studies. As in the case of all Council publications, statements of fact and expressions of opinion contained in 1980s Project Studies are the sole responsibility of their authors.

The editors of this book were Lucy Despard, Amy Litt, and Thomas E. Wallin for the Council on Foreign Relations. Thomas Quinn and Michael Hennelly were the editors for McGraw-Hill Book Company. Christopher Simon was the designer, and Teresa Leaden supervised the production. This book was set in Times Roman by Offset Composition Services, Inc.

Printed and bound by R. R. Donnelley and Sons.

**Library of Congress Cataloging in Publication Data**
Main entry under title:

Africa in the 1980s.

(1980s Project/Council on Foreign Relations)
Bibliography: p.
Includes index.
1.  Africa—Politics and government—1960–
Addresses, essays, lectures.   2.   Africa—Economic
conditions—1945– Addresses, essays, lectures.
I.  Legum, Colin.   II.  Title.   III.  Series: Council on
Foreign Relations.   1980s Project/Council on Foreign
Relations.
DT30.A347          320.9′6′03          78-11649
ISBN 0-07-037081-8
ISBN 0-07-037082-6 pbk.

1 2 3 4 5 6 7 8 9 R R D R R D 7 9 8 0 3 2 1 0 9

# Contents

078412

# CONTENTS

# Foreword: The 1980s Project

These explorations of the likely paths of economic and political development in the nations of Subsaharan, Africa, of the roles that African states might play in world politics, and of the vulnerability of the African continent to outside intervention are part of a stream of studies commissioned by the 1980s Project of the Council on Foreign Relations. Each Project study analyzes an issue or set of issues that is likely to be of international concern during the next 10 to 20 years.

The ambitious purpose of the 1980s Project is to examine important political and economic problems not only individually but in relationship to one another. Some studies or books produced by the Project will primarily emphasize the interrelationship of issues. In the case of other, more specifically focused studies, a considerable effort has been made to write, review, and criticize them in the context of more general Project work. Each Project study is thus capable of standing on its own; at the same time it has been shaped by a broader perspective.

The 1980s Project had its origin in the widely held recognition that many of the assumptions, policies, and institutions that have characterized international relations during the past 30 years are inadequate to the demands of today and the foreseeable demands of the period between now and 1990 or so. Over the course of the next decade, substantial adaptation of institutions and behavior will be needed to respond to the changed circumstances of the 1980s and beyond. The Project seeks to identify those future conditions and the kinds of adaptation they might require. It is not the Project's purpose to arrive at a single or exclusive set of goals. Nor does it focus upon the foreign policy or national interests of the United States alone. Instead, it seeks to identify goals that are compatible with the perceived interests of most states, despite differences in ideology and in level of economic development.

The published products of the Project are aimed at a broad readership, including policy makers and potential policy makers and those who would influence the policy-making process, but are confined to no single nation or region. The authors of Project studies were therefore asked to remain mindful of interests broader than those of any one society and to take fully into account the likely realities of domestic politics in the principal societies involved. All those who have worked on the Project, however, have tried not to be captives of the status quo; they have sought to question the inevitability of existing patterns of thought and behavior that restrain desirable change and to look for ways in which those patterns might in time be altered or their consequences mitigated.

The 1980s Project is at once a series of separate attacks upon a number of urgent and potentially urgent international problems and also a collective effort, involving a substantial number of persons in the United States and abroad, to bring those separate approaches to bear upon one another and to suggest the kinds of choices that might be made among them. The Project involves more than 300 participants. A small central staff and a steering Coordinating Group have worked to define the questions and to assess the compatibility of policy prescriptions. Nearly 100 authors, from more than a dozen countries, have been at work on separate studies. Ten working groups of specialists and generalists have been convened to subject the Project's studies to critical scrutiny and to help in the process of identifying interrelationships among them.

The 1980s Project is the largest single research and studies effort the Council on Foreign Relations has undertaken in its 55-year history, comparable in conception only to a major study of the postwar world, the War and Peace Studies, undertaken by the Council during the Second World War. At that time, the impetus of the effort was the discontinuity caused by worldwide conflict and the visible and inescapable need to rethink, replace, and supplement many of the features of the international system that had prevailed before the war. The discontinuities in today's world are less obvious and, even when occasionally quite visible—as in the abandonment of gold convertibility and fixed monetary parities—only briefly command the spotlight of public attention. That new institutions and patterns of behavior are needed in many areas is widely acknowledged, but the sense of need is less urgent—existing institutions have not for the most part dramatically failed and collapsed. The tendency, therefore, is to make do with outmoded arrangements and to improvise rather than to undertake a basic analysis of the problems that lie before us and of the demands that those problems will place upon all nations.

The 1980s Project is based upon the belief that serious effort and integrated forethought can contribute—indeed, are indispensable—to progress in the next decade toward a more humane, peaceful, productive, and just world. And it rests upon the hope that participants in its deliberations and readers of Project publications—whether or not they agree with an author's point of view—may be helped to think more informedly about the opportunities and the dangers that lie ahead and the consequences of various possible courses of future action.

The 1980s Project has been made possible by generous grants from the Ford Foundation, the Lilly Endowment, the Andrew W. Mellon Foundation, the Rockefeller Foundation, and the German Marshall Fund of the United States. Neither the Council on Foreign Relations nor any of those foundations is responsible for statements of fact and expressions of opinion contained in publications of the 1980s Project; they are the sole responsibility of the individual authors under whose names they appear. But the Council on Foreign Relations and the staff of the 1980s Project take great pleasure in placing those publications before a wide readership both in the United States and abroad.

## 1980s PROJECT WORKING GROUPS

During 1975 and 1976, ten Working Groups met to explore major international issues and to subject initial drafts of 1980s Project studies to critical review. Those who chaired Project Working Groups were:

*Cyrus R. Vance*, Working Group on Nuclear Weapons and Other Weapons of Mass Destruction

*Leslie H. Gelb*, Working Group on Armed Conflict

*Roger Fisher*, Working Group on Transnational Violence and Subversion

*Rev. Theodore M. Hesburgh*, Working Group on Human Rights

*Joseph S. Nye, Jr.*, Working Group on the Political Economy of North-South Relations

*Harold Van B. Cleveland*, Working Group on Macroeconomic Policies and International Monetary Relations

*Lawrence C. McQuade*, Working Group on Principles of International Trade

*William Diebold, Jr.*, Working Group on Multinational Enterprises

*Eugene B. Skolnikoff*, Working Group on the Environment, the Global Commons, and Economic Growth

*Miriam Camps*, Working Group on Industrial Policy

## 1980s PROJECT STAFF

Persons who have held senior professional positions on the staff of the 1980s Project for all or part of its duration are:

| | |
|---|---|
| *Miriam Camps* | *Catherine Gwin* |
| *William Diebold, Jr.* | *Roger D. Hansen* |
| *Tom J. Farer* | *Edward L. Morse* |
| *David C. Gompert* | *Richard H. Ullman* |

Richard H. Ullman was Director of the 1980s Project from its inception in 1974 until July 1977, when he became Chairman of the Project Coordinating Group. Edward L. Morse was Executive Director from July 1977 until June 1978. At that time, Catherine Gwin, 1980s Project Fellow since 1976, took over as Executive Director.

## PROJECT COORDINATING GROUP

The Coordinating Group of the 1980s had a central advisory role in the work of the Project. Its members as of June 30, 1978, were:

*Carlos F. Díaz-Alejandro*       *Bayless Manning*
*Richard A. Falk*                *Theodore R. Marmor*
*Tom J. Farer*                   *Ali Mazrui*
*Edward K. Hamilton*             *Michael O'Neill*
*Stanley Hoffmann*               *Stephen Stamas*
*Gordon J. MacDonald*            *Fritz Stern*
*Bruce K. MacLaury*              *Allen S. Whiting*

Until they entered government service, other members included:

*W. Michael Blumenthal*          *Joseph S. Nye, Jr.*
*Richard N. Cooper*              *Marshall D. Shulman*
*Samuel P. Huntington*

## COMMITTEE ON STUDIES

The Committee on Studies of the Board of Directors of the Council on Foreign Relations is the governing body of the 1980s Project. The Committee's members as of June 30, 1978, were:

*Barry E. Carter*               *Robert E. Osgood*
*Robert A. Charpie*             *Stephen Stamas*
*Stanley Hoffmann*              *Paul A. Volcker*
*Henry A. Kissinger*            *Marina v. N. Whitman*
*Walter J. Levy*
*James A. Perkins (Chairman)*

xii

**Africa, 1979**

# Africa in the 1980s

# Introduction: International Involvement in a Changing Africa

Catherine Gwin

The African countries, having gained formal independence in the 1960s and 1970s, face difficult tasks in the building of durable and self-reliant nation-states. These tasks—which involve substantial social and economic change as well as the construction of responsive public institutions—will pose grave problems for both African societies and the international system in the decade of the 1980s.

Cleavages between clans, tribes, and nations are likely to remain a seriously disruptive force in domestic and regional politics. Sensitive border disputes—one of the troubling legacies of colonialism—threaten periodically to erupt into armed conflict. An intransigent system of racism in South Africa may lead to an extended war. Moreover, many countries are likely to experience a widening gap between rich and poor segments of their societies, a rise in urban and rural unemployment or underemployment, and a deepening of mass poverty.

Although the major burdens of coping with such problems will lie with the African nations themselves, outsiders will continue to shape the environment within which the tasks of nation building must proceed, their actions weighing heavily on chances for accelerating growth and averting impending crises. Most important, perhaps, avoiding escalation of internal or regional disputes is likely to depend as much on the readiness of outside powers to exercise restraint in pursuit of competitive interests in Africa as on the willingness of African states to act together to bring about peaceful resolution of local disputes. Prospects for peaceful development do not appear promising. Indeed, ethnic conflicts and the struggle for political power in African states threaten to draw rival foreign powers into intensified competition for political and military influence in the region.

The studies in this volume explore these problems and other constraints on development in Africa. Each looks at a different set of issues and draws different conclusions about the probable course of development through the 1980s. In the first study, Colin Legum, associate editor of the London *Observer*, assesses prospects for continuing ethnic conflict within and among African states and for increased involvement by major outside powers in these conflicts. In the second study, I. William Zartman, professor of political science at New York University, focuses on the politics of managing scarce domestic resources and looks to improvements in Africa's position in the world economy as a driving force for development. However, as Zartman indicates, political struggles in southern Africa are likely to play a major role in shaping the future of Africa's ties to outside powers and, hence, its future development prospects. Arguing that the international economic relations of African states will continue to impede rather than promote national development, Steven Langdon and Lynn Mytelka, professors at Carleton University in Ottawa, conclude in the third study that pressures within African states will force many governments to turn toward more inward-looking or self-reliant strategies of development.

These three studies comprise one of five volumes in the 1980s Project that analyze economic and political trends in the principal regions of the developing world. Each volume explores regional prospects for sustained economic development over the next 10 to 15 years, the extent to which regional cooperation will become a major feature of growth and development strategies, and how, in the pursuit of national objectives, the states of the different regions will choose to relate to other countries of the industrial "North" and the developing "South." Each volume is designed to stand on its own as a projective analysis of a distinct region, and each volume fits into the overall effort of the 1980s Project to analyze and prescribe ways of handling some of the major issues likely to be the subject of international contention in the decade of the 1980s and beyond.

## STATE AND NATION BUILDING IN AFRICA

At stake in the African states are the legitimacy of governments that came to power through the transfer of formal authority at the end of the long era of colonialism, the unity of communities delineated by the arbitrary drawing of colonial borders, and the prosperity of economies that are among the least developed and, in many cases, the poorest in the world. The power that national leaders gained in the struggle against colonialism has not proven easy to translate into effective public institutions with broad authority. Nor has the solidarity forged among diverse ethnic groups in struggles for independence held together everywhere in the postindependence era. Societies remain fragmented and economic development limited.

As Colin Legum explains, the intricate and complex patterns of cultural affinities that endure in—and rend asunder—the societies of Africa are one factor impeding the processes of national integration. Increasing competition for control over national economic and political resources within each of these societies has heightened ethnic self-consciousness, and violent conflicts have proliferated. In some states, as in the case of Burundi, national elites have engaged in massive acts of official violence to preempt challenges to their rule. Elsewhere, as in the Horn of Africa, ethnic groups have tried to forge a nation out of ethnically affiliated people who live on two sides of a national border. In other cases, such as Zaire, diverse clans and tribes that see themselves as oppressed or disenfranchised minorities or majorities have sought to defend their separate interests against the encroachments of ruling national groups by waging wars of secession aimed at the establishment of an ethnic state or by instigating civil conflicts to gain control over the instruments of state.

How well the African states will be able to cope with these kinds of strains in the future will depend largely on the ability of a new generation of postindependence leaders to foster a sense

3

of common purpose among the ethnically diverse and burgeoning populations. And this question, in turn, will depend heavily on their ability to design innovative development strategies that provide for sharing of the benefits of economic growth among ethnic and other socioeconomic groups. Both efforts—of nation building and of national economic development—will confront the governments with difficult choices about their relations with outside states. In essence, for these governments there is a tension between pursuit of domestic gains through international means, on the one hand, and through national autonomy, on the other. There are political and economic opportunities and constraints attendant on each.

A notable feature in African states, indeed in developing countries generally, is the central role of the state in the process of social change. While the content and direction of that change vary considerably from government to government, a common characteristic is the emergence of some version of authoritarian rule and state-led growth.[1] There is little evidence that in Africa the 1980s will witness a weakening of will by national elites to further consolidate and expand this role and—as they anticipate—the political and economic strength of their countries.

In times past, the process of constructing a national public authority that could unify the various social groups was aided by the reign of dynastic rulers who managed not only to centralize power but also to become the embodiment of a nation. In the late twentieth century, hereditary dynasties are no longer a political option. The oldest African dynasty, in Ethiopia, has been overthrown, and the newest, the Central African Empire, seems destined to be short-lived. A modern alternative is the monolithic political party headed by a strong and charismatic leader; however, the future of single-party rule appears uncertain. The fall of Kwame Nkrumah brought the collapse of Ghana's single party. And, except in Mozambique and other new socialist regimes, it seems doubtful that other dominant single parties will survive the deaths of independence leaders such as Kenya's Kenyatta, Senegal's Senghor, or Guinea's Sékou Touré.

[1]These ideas were developed in a background paper by Riordan Roett for a 1980s Project working group on North-South relations.

The military might be said to represent an alternative national unifying force. Where the military has taken power it has sought to organize and consolidate the instruments of state. But there is a crucial difference between a state and a nation, and most military leaders—often members of a single cultural group—have done little to cement national unity in the independent African states. Indeed, military state building has been based more often on the repressive use of official violence than on the mobilization of popular support and responsiveness to public demands. Actions designed to maintain governmental stability in the short term have taken precedence over efforts aimed at building social harmony in the long run. This process of maintaining "social peace" in the absence of political development has tended to lead governments to rely heavily on outsiders for the economic and military support needed to maintain stability and retain power.

In the "dependency" school of thought, the rise of authoritarian rule and of state control over the economy is explained by the workings of the international system, which is seen as the key factor determining the structural features of the South's regimes. To what extent the "imperatives of dependency" actually shape the political institutions of developing countries is a subject of considerable current debate, which need not concern us here. What is pertinent is that the increasing role of the state in national development needs to be understood in the context of other givens: economic dependence, the prominent role of international capital and multinational corporations in developing economies, the alliance of interests of national elites and foreign economic actors, and, in Africa, the recent history of decolonization.

The predominant characteristics of the new authoritarianism in Africa and elsewhere in the Third World are (1) a heavy reliance on bureaucratic decision making, (2) a major role for the state in national development planning, (3) compliance of labor and entrepreneurs in state-directed modernization, and (4) an extremely limited, however varied, form of public participation in the politics of development. What is important to the performance and continuing vitality of contemporary authoritarian regimes is that the regimes are dynamic, not static. The capacity

5

and will of centralized governments to implement social change of one form or another—and with a greater or a lesser degree of equity—may be stronger in the states of, say, Latin America, where political institutions are relatively less fragile and ethnic diversity somewhat less a source of strife, than in Africa, but the expected role of the state in African economic and social development is no less central.

As a factor in that dynamism, the driving force of state-led growth has tended to involve a growing economic nationalism. That is, the desire for increased independence has led governments to assert their authority over the productive capacities of the state and the basic natural resources of the nation. While this form of economic nationalism is somewhat less in evidence in Africa than in the more highly industrialized economies of Latin America, which have gained an economic strength and political coherence to alter significantly their bargaining position with economic actors of the North, it is a trend that may increase on the continent through the coming decade. For the authoritarian regimes in Africa there are costs of enhanced autonomy to be weighed against the costs of continued dependence.

In political terms, the issue is one of freedom of maneuver for a government in both its domestic and its foreign policy decision making. This objective may be of particular importance to a society undergoing major structural changes. However, as the Legum study suggests, the weighing of political trade-offs between autonomy and dependence is especially problematic for a government confronted by limited national unity and open to serious disputes with neighboring states. Greater autonomy is sought as an attribute of national sovereignty and for the improved economic bargaining strength that it is assumed to afford. Yet its attainment would put increased pressure on governments to respond more effectively to domestic demands. It would likely create pressure for improved regional relations since few developing states can afford to wage war with their neighbors without access to concessional transfers of arms and other military support. The dilemma of choosing is compounded by the fact that the building of responsive domestic institutions and regional cooperation would themselves entail constraints on any government's freedom of maneuver. This tension between stability and autonomy is not likely to be easy to resolve where outside powers react to continuing ethnic and other local political conflicts as opportunities for advancing their own national interests.

The many unresolved political disputes of the postcolonial era in Africa and the struggle for black rule in southern Africa "invite intervention." Governments of independent African states seek increasing amounts of military and economic support from outside powers. And outsiders, with a mix of political, economic, and strategic interests on the continent, seek to affect the outcome of internal and intrastate conflicts.

The superpowers and their allies have different national economic and strategic interests at stake in Africa. The United States and Western Europe share an interest in preventing the Soviet Union from establishing itself as an important military actor in the continent and the surrounding oceans. They share an economic interest in ensuring that they are not deprived of access to Africa's strategic resources by Soviet-inspired national policies. They serve these interests by giving military and economic aid to key states. At the same time they have competitive economic interests in those African countries that appear to offer profitable markets and investment locations.

The Soviet Union has recently displayed an increased strategic interest in establishing a network of naval and air facilities in Africa to enhance its own role as a new world naval power. It also has an interest in counteracting China's growing influence in the continent. It seeks to achieve these strategic and political aims (as well as to strengthen its trading position) by encouraging the development of Marxist regimes in Africa. This the Soviet Union is now doing—much as the West seeks to sustain clients— by giving military and political as well as economic support to favored governments. It has also demonstrated its readiness to give similar support in some instances to opposition political forces.

Although the Soviet Union has not demonstrated a capacity or willingness to extend developmental assistance on a large scale, it appears now to see the possibility of making major political gains in Africa by transferring economic and military aid, with the help of Cuba, to conflict-ridden and conflict-prone parts of the continent. Such a build-up of Soviet influence, if directly countered by an equivalent intensification of Western involvement in areas in conflict, not only threatens détente and complicates chances for the peaceful resolution of disputes among African parties but also is likely to inhibit movement toward greater international cooperation on a number of issues of global importance including, in particular, efforts to control the transfer of arms.

Already the intensifying competition among outsiders in Africa is producing a rapid growth in the transfer of conventional arms on both commercial and concessional terms. In a context of local instability and uneven distribution of power, requests for supply of arms and military training raise fundamental questions of security, order, and justice. Critics of today's arms trade argue that transfers feed local arms races, heighten regional tensions, and jeopardize regional power equilibriums, thereby raising risks of local war. The purchase of arms from abroad by developing states, they further maintain, is a tragic waste of scarce resources. Yet opponents of this view stress that arms transfers can help correct regional power imbalances by shoring up weak states threatened by homegrown or foreign-backed regional powers or by equipping states within the developing world to resist intervention and intimidation by external powers.[2]

A strong regional leadership or a concerted regional effort could perhaps damp the spread of weapons. But in Africa there is little or no regional capacity to deter outside interference in local disputes, despite the expressed general desire of African leaders to avoid new waves of foreign intervention and domination. Strongly divisive forces also keep regionalism at bay. The Organization of African Unity (OAU), formed in the early 1960s, has publicly come out against any foreign intervention in domestic or regional disputes, and some of its members—including Tanzania—have strongly argued this point with the So-

[2]For an extended projective and prescriptive analysis of future arms transfers see the 1980s Project volume, by Anne Hessing Cahn et al., *Controlling Future Arms Trade*, McGraw-Hill for the Council on Foreign Relations, New York, 1977.

viet Union and the West. Norms of nonintervention do in other words exist, and they are likely to be increasingly stressed in the future. However, the OAU has no authority or mechanism to act in the event of internal conflicts even where they may have serious international complications. And the Organization has not yet developed an authoritative capability for conflict management or dispute settlement. Such key states as Nigeria, Algeria, and Egypt have only begun to consolidate their power and to establish an effective regional leadership role. It is not yet clear that their emergence as regional powers will bring peace and progressive stability rather than new rivalries, conflict, and further competitive foreign penetration. Thus, while the process of strengthening or building regional machinery to reduce potential conflicts among neighboring states could be as important a component as national integration in constructing progressive and self-reliant societies in the coming decade, chances for overcoming the many intraregional factors that inhibit peaceful relations and setting limitations on a regional arms race are apt to depend primarily on factors outside the region, the evolution of the "rules of détente" being a major factor.

Growing competition among outside powers for political and military influence in Africa is likely to be little more compatible with promotion of human rights than it is with control of conventional arms transfers. In general, worldwide concern over violations of human rights has raised a number of difficult questions about how outsiders—individuals, governments, and international institutions—can bring influence to bear to cause genuine and lasting improvements in the treatment of individuals by governments. Currently those (from Western democratic societies for the most part) who are seeking international action in support of human rights concern themselves primarily with certain egregious violations against individual physical security (genocide, torture, summary execution) and traditional political rights (freedom of speech and assembly). But there are also economic rights—sometimes labeled "human needs"—which include those aspects of existence necessary to secure the basic development of the human being (adequate nutrition, housing, health care, and education).

Those who emphasize basic needs contend that their assurance or deprivation is just as much a subject for, and a result of, state policy as is the provision of traditional civil and political rights. When, either through negligence or through deliberate acts of policy, governments deny the basic needs of persons living within the territory they control, they violate human rights just as surely as they violate the rights of political opponents whom they muzzle or jail. When any rights are violated, however, the problem remains of how concerned parties can induce a government to modify its behavior.

Governments do not indulge casually in egregious violations of human rights. Rather, as noted in another 1980s volume, "they do so because they fear that they will be deflected from the pursuit of programs which they judge to be in their own interests . . . or in the interests of their entire societies."[3] Thus in few cases will there be any scope for effective, minimal cost leverage brought by outsiders. Deterioration of relations with a previously or potentially "friendly" government is more likely.

In the African context the question of how outsiders can effect change has particular importance, given both the absence of any regional machinery with the power and authority to come to the aid of victims of a brutal regime like Idi Amin's and the existence of the system of institutionalized racism that persists in South Africa.

## THE SPECIAL PROBLEM OF SOUTH AFRICA

"Overwhelming everything else in Africa," President Nyerere of Tanzania has written, "is the sense of nationalism and the determination of all African peoples that the whole of this continent shall be free and relieved from the humiliation of organized white racialism." By the 1980s it is likely that this determination will be sharply focused on one area: South Africa. In Zimbabwe and Namibia, black majorities will likely be in control by the end

[3]Richard H. Ullman, "Human Rights: Toward International Action," in Domínguez et al., *Enhancing Global Human Rights*, McGraw-Hill for the Council on Foreign Relations/1980s Project, New York, 1979.

of the current decade and disputes among rival black factions might well be resolved. After that both international and external pressures for change in South Africa will intensify.

How the transfer to majority rule is accomplished in Zimbabwe and Namibia will have an important impact on relations throughout the rest of the continent and, most importantly, on the course of events in South Africa. A protracted armed conflict in Zimbabwe after failure to negotiate a just political settlement would strain relations among black-ruled African states—especially in the South—and would, in all likelihood, deeply involve outside powers on the sides of contending political forces. Such a conflict might also undermine whatever chances for peaceful change exist in South Africa. The two scenarios portraying alternative paths to change in southern Africa that William Zartman sketches out at the end of his study aptly demonstrate this tight interrelationship between the attainment of majority rule in Zimbabwe and the racial struggle in South Africa.

Even with the achievement of a political settlement that is acceptable to all parties in Zimbabwe, no area of the continent is likely to pose graver dangers of extended war in the coming decade than South Africa, and no area of the world is likely to pose more starkly questions regarding the role of foreign powers and global institutions in opposing gross injustices and inhumanities. South Africa is likely to become this "special problem" not because injustice and inhumanity in South Africa are unique, but because of South Africa's unique system of institutionalized racism in which injustice and inhumanity are statutorily enshrined.

At issue in South Africa is the future of a system of apartheid—now called "separate development"—that by force of draconian law and repressive actions sustains the economic and political dominance of a white minority over a large black majority. Not only are the blacks of South Africa excluded from participation in national political life, but they are officially treated in every way as an inferior race. There is evidence that egregious violations of individual security, integrity, and well-being are integral to the maintenance of the system of official racism.

For many years the existence of generally favorable economic

11

conditions within South Africa and of friendly governments on the country's borders made it possible for the white government to ignore the problems of the basic artificiality and instability of the system of apartheid. And, in the absence of sustained internal strife, the indignities of the system were largely ignored by the world at large. As conditions change within and outside southern Africa, however, there is likely to be growing pressure on the Pretorian government from those who oppose its racist policies, "internal colonialism," and abuse of basic human rights.

Some observers assert that the existing government now recognizes that the country is facing a major crisis and that changes will have to come. But time may be running short on chances for peaceful change. How far and how fast the government is prepared—or can be encouraged—to move is not clear. Consequently, various actions by outside parties have been proposed as means of exerting pressure on the white government not only to remove the most repugnant features of its system of racial discrimination but also to share political power justly.

Proposals made by those still hopeful about the chances for inducing peaceful change range from unilateral expressions of disapproval to an array of international economic and political sanctions designed to ostracize and undermine the South African government. While the Soviet Union and its ally, Cuba, can act to affect the situation in South Africa through arming and assisting black "liberation" forces, it is the industrialized countries of the West that must choose whether or not to try to exert pressure for peaceful change, for it is the West alone that has substantial enough economic links to have a bearing on the future well-being of the whites and their regime. It remains to be seen whether sufficient consensus will emerge on which to build stronger action. Several countries within and outside Africa— notably Great Britain, but also Zambia, Zimbabwe, and Mozambique—have substantial economic links with South Africa and would be considerably affected by the imposition of economic sanctions against Pretoria. To enlist the support of those states that in the short run would be paying the highest price for sanctions against South Africa may require some kind of international arrangement on "burden sharing." There is, however, no precedent, nor yet an expression of the political will for exerting the kind of large-scale international action that seems required to make an impact on the intransigent white government.

It is frequently argued that pressure on the white regime for change will only lead to a hunkering down on the part of the whites. Nonetheless it seems abundantly clear that movement toward a just and peaceful world order cannot forever sidestep the persistence of racism and political oppression in South Africa. Change will come in South Africa—through peaceful or violent means—and outside powers will be involved. The nature of that involvement will affect not only the character of the nation-state that emerges but also the state of relations that prevails for many years thereafter among African nations and between them and the rest of the world.

## MARSHALING RESOURCES FOR DEVELOPMENT

While political struggles in southern Africa and elsewhere on the continent are heightening the involvement of outside powers in African affairs, problems of economic development are propelling African states to search for new modes of foreign economic relations. This attempt to gain greater control over the future of their economies and increased returns from economic activities has allied black African states with other Third World countries in a drive to compel the establishment of a New International Economic Order. Through concerted action the developing countries of the South aim to alter their aid, trade, and investment relations with the industrialized countries of the North and gain for themselves a greater voice in the management of international economic and political affairs. This aim has led to demands for special preferential treatment in trade, a Common Fund to finance a series of international commodity agreements, improved access to industrial technology, and increases in aid on better and more automatic terms.

Although the second and third studies in this volume are based on different lines of analysis, they both reach the conclusion that other measures not now at the center of North-South negotiations

Wingate College Library

are needed to spur rapid and peaceful development in Africa. They both suggest that to overcome poverty and underdevelopment in Africa there must be some change in the development policies and priorities of most African states. A few states, Zartman notes, may achieve accelerated rates of economic growth over the course of the next 10 to 15 years, but many face crises of potentially monumental proportions—including serious chronic shortages of food—which can be met only by a shift in emphasis away from "top-heavy" industrial development.

The argument for new directions in development is one that has been building over the last several years both within and outside the developing world. It is animated by increasing evidence that historically unprecedented rates of growth in many parts of the developing world are being accompanied by a persistent or worsening incidence of poverty. Disheartened by the outcome of the conventional "trickle-down" approach to development and growth, new strategies have been advanced that call for "growth with equity" or "redistribution with growth."[4]

At the core of recommendations for a new approach to development is a concern with "righting imbalances"[5] among sectors, regions, and individuals. Achieving this would require a shift in the allocation of resources in favor of agriculture and the rural poor (who comprise roughly 80 percent of the total population in developing countries). It would also entail the adoption of measures explicitly designed to increase productive employment. In societies where the bulk of the population works on the land or in the informal sectors of the economy rather than in

[4]See, for example, the study by Hollis B. Chenery et al., *Redistribution with Growth*, Oxford University Press for the World Bank, London, 1974; International Labour Organization, *Employment, Growth and Basic Needs*, Geneva, 1976; and the 1980s Project study by Roger D. Hansen, *Beyond the North-South Stalemate*, McGraw-Hill for the Council on Foreign Relations, New York, 1979.

[5]A strategy for achieving growth with equity in one African country, Kenya, is set out in a lengthy report made by a team of international labor investigators. The report, entitled *Employment, Incomes and Equity: A Strategy for Increasing Productive Employment in Kenya*, International Labour Organization, Geneva, 1972, remains one of the most important discussions of a new approach for development in Africa.

wage-earning jobs, this means a focus not exclusively on the generation of jobs but also on improving opportunities for earning more reasonable incomes through more equitable access to education, land, credit, and other assets. Such efforts would be designed to alter the distribution of new income, thereby increasing the purchasing power and effective demand of the poor. Additionally a range of other policy measures is called for by some development economists more directly to provide basic goods (such as food, shelter, and medicine) and services (including clean water, sewage facilities, education) to the currently deprived segments of each developing society.

While there is broad agreement on the most essential components of a new, more equitable, and sustainable strategy of growth, there is sharp disagreement on whether "growth with equity" should be an inward-looking or an outward-looking strategy. The authors of the second and third studies in this volume differ on this point. Reflected in their *contrary* assessments are differing views about where the obstacles to and forces of change lie.

The main constraint on development in Africa, Zartman indicates, is the sheer scarcity of available resources with which to meet diverse and growing social demands. The problem of the management of scarce resources is as much one of politics as of economics. There is an enormous gap between what is expected of governments and what authorities can foster in providing gains to individual welfare, economic growth, and national security. This gap augments the difficulty of constructing durable public institutions. In the context of scarcity, the Zartman study suggests, the promise of development lies in the attainment of increased resource gains on improved terms from accelerated integration into the global economy.

Langdon and Mytelka argue, however, that it is not the *absence* of resources so much as which interests control how resources are used that keeps African societies "underdeveloped." African social and economic development is constrained, they contend, by the dependence of the African economies on external economic forces and, more particularly, by the ability of multinational corporations—which dominate the modern sectors of the

15

local economies—to shape the use of resources in their own best interest. While these interests are compatible with those of a narrow group of economic elite in the host countries, their influence distorts the development process. Both policies of industrialization through import substitution and limited efforts at regional integration, undertaken as measures to accelerate growth in the 1960s and 1970s, enhanced the position of multinationals in Africa. These policies reinforced the internal structural constraints to development that derive from continued foreign economic dependence. They have not reduced inequalities, nor have they provided the foundation for self-reliant development. Nor, the authors explain, will the special trade and aid arrangements negotiated with the European Economic Community (EEC) or under negotiation in the North-South dialogue be sufficient to break the vicious circle of underdevelopment that entraps the majority of Africans. The real problem, Langdon and Mytelka indicate, has to do with what is produced, how, and for whom.

Skeptical of chances for extensive change in the structure of international economic relations and wary of the effect that any likely changes will have on prospects for development, Langdon and Mytelka conclude that mounting pressures of underdevelopment will force African states to adopt more self-reliant strategies of development. In short, they suggest that these pressures will—and should—force African countries to "delink" from the international economic system. They see these pressures for change coming from within the underdeveloped societies as a response to obstacles to change that derive from the "internationalization" of the African economies.

What, one might ask, are the chances that the African states will choose a self-reliant path to development? What would be the costs of that choice? While self-reliance is not synonymous with autarky, an inward-looking strategy necessarily puts added pressure on governments to mobilize both material and political domestic resources. As suggested above, the strategy would require in the African context much improved relations among neighboring states. Legum's portrayal of the depth of ethnic divisiveness and the intensification of outside interests in the region, together with Zartman's accounting of the scarcity of resources upon which leaders can draw, would, it seems, militate against a major advance toward self-reliance in the coming decade.

Yet it is difficult to see in the outward-looking approach to development the dynamics of change that will bring about a more equitable sharing of the benefits of economic growth. At the international level "collective bargaining" by the developing states may lead to increased gains for some countries and for some people within those countries. But it is not clear that the African states stand to gain as much as some of the more advanced Third World countries, nor that what little gains are made will have a positive effect on the poorest people in the poorest countries. For the oil-exporting states in Africa, Algeria and Nigeria, a significant transfer of resources is being made through the price actions of OPEC. For some other raw material exporters, including copper-rich Zaire, an international buffer stock scheme might lead to more stable, if not higher, export earnings. Yet what most African economies need more than price-stabilizing schemes for some well-established raw material exports— of which they are not the leading producers—is a substantial and continuing flow of resources into agricultural diversification and other development efforts. Since few African countries have the economic standing to borrow heavily from private capital sources or the wherewithal to handle greatly increased levels of international indebtedness, this suggests the need for increased foreign aid in the form of both technical assistance and capital flows on improved concessionary terms.

The special problems of the African states were made clear in the fall of 1977, when negotiations were postponed on the establishment of a Common Fund for commodity-export price stabilization, in part as a result of the efforts of the group of African states within the Southern coalition to expand the envisaged functions of the Fund beyond the financing of buffer stocks to include general financing of development projects. The African states, recognizing that they had relatively little to gain from the specific buffer stock arrangements under negotiation, insisted that proposals for the Fund put forth by the Group of

77 allow for the use of the Fund for activities other than market stabilization. This proposal would have required a far larger Common Fund than the North was prepared to support, and negotiations broke off. It is likely that a commodity fund acceptable in design and plan of implementation to both North and South would not have been possible under any circumstances in 1977, but the general point regarding the compatibility of needs and priorities of the different groups of states within the coalition of the South has relevance beyond the 1970s and the issue of the Common Fund.

African states have achieved more substantial progress on a number of economic issues within the narrower context of their negotiations with the European Community. Under the most recent Lomé Convention—negotiated jointly by the African, Caribbean, and Pacific (ACP) countries associated with the European Community—agreement was reached on, among other things, improved market access for many products originating in the ACP states and on an export-earnings-stabilization scheme (STABEX) that converts stabilization loans into grants for the poorest countries in years of successive export-earning declines. The gains on export-earnings stabilization, aid, and access to the markets of industrial countries have come at considerable expense, however, to the African states' national autonomy and freedom of maneuver. For instance, the STABEX system is a disincentive to those countries to further process commodities prior to export. And the Lomé Convention involves rules for improved market access designed to guarantee preferential rights of establishment for EEC multinational firms vis-à-vis their Japanese and American competitors. Moreover, the measures designed to increase the African states' foreign-exchange earnings have reinforced rather than reformed the existing development policies that have allowed for the perpetuation of mass poverty.

Consideration of the many trade-offs between autonomy and interdependence—illuminated clearly by the studies in this volume—suggests that whether or not the pressures of poverty and internal inequities push the African states away from a strategy of outward-looking growth and toward self-reliance may depend in the future on whether there develops international consensus

18

on the desirability of eliminating poverty worldwide and, therefore, the pattern of economic relations among poor and rich states
is changed.[6] In the current political climate of stalemated negotiations between the industrialized North and developing
South, it is difficult to imagine that such a view will come to
prevail. Indeed, states of the South are suspicious of proposals
from the North to shape international development assistance
to help countries meet basic needs. The proposals appear to the
South to be an attempt on the part of the North to divert attention
from international economic restructuring. Besides, spokesmen
for the South contend, states should be left to determine their
own development priorities.

Nonetheless, significant new attention is being given to food
as a world problem and a central aspect of global poverty. Since
hunger is a function of poverty, and poverty a function of under-
or uneven development, concern over world hunger as a mani-
festation of poverty leads to increased attention to constraints
on development. A focus on problems of food insufficiency and
hunger also points up the need for reform and innovation in
international development programs. When attention shifts away
from a definition of development as aggregate economic growth
stimulated by a transfer of resources from abroad to a view of
development as growth with equity, greater emphasis falls on
the internal policies of developing states and, in turn, on the need
for new forms of cooperation for development that conform to
the broad needs and build on the initiative of the developing
countries.

One attempt to devise innovative forms of assistance is already
under way in a particularly poor and vulnerable subregion of
Africa: the Sahel. Spurred by the devastating famine that swept
through this central part of the continent in the mid-1970s, Sa-

[6]Several other studies in the 1980s Project discuss the relation between
restructuring of international economic relations and the elimination of poverty
worldwide. They include Albert Fishlow et al., *Rich and Poor Nations in the
World Economy*, McGraw-Hill for the Council on Foreign Relations, New
York, 1978; Roger D. Hansen, *Beyond the North-South Stalemate*; and a
forthcoming study by Miriam Camps and Catherine Gwin on managing change
in an interdependent world.

helian governments and interested multilateral- and bilateral-aid donors joined together in a "Club du Sahel" to mount an action-oriented development program. Noteworthy features of the Club du Sahel include its objective, timetable, and mode of operation. Its aim is to integrate local and international resources to implement a primary goal: food self-sufficiency. The "Sahel Development Plan" designed to achieve this goal covers a 20-year period and is built upon coordinated action programs drawn up by multilateral working groups, each headed by a Sahelian and composed of donor and recipient representatives.

It might also be noted that the Sahelian effort is organized on a loose, subregional basis, which is the geographic dimension that Zartman predicts will form the predominant pattern of inter-African relations in the medium-term future and will be the level for significant negotiation with the North. It may be that the Club could serve as a model for joint long-term subregional development programs elsewhere. But it is far from clear that the 1980s will bring the important improvements in relations among neighboring African states, or the expansion and coordination of international development assistance efforts required to make Sahelian-type experiments work.

Clearly, none of the issues raised in this introduction is uniquely relevant to Africa as distinct from other developing regions. But the potential crises that the studies in this volume suggest will loom large in Africa's future make the search for ways of dealing with each one of them a pressing matter for both African states and the international community.

# Communal Conflict and International Intervention in Africa

Colin Legum

# Introduction

Virtually no nation-states yet exist in Africa. The continental political systems are at different stages of evolution toward becoming, or possibly failing to become, viable nation-states. Almost none of the 50-odd African countries possesses the degree of homogeneity that would facilitate conflict-free national integration. The only possible exceptions include Egypt, Tunisia, Morocco, Lesotho, and Somalia. Most of the other African states are characterized by cultural cleavages of varying intensity.

Africa is in a historical period analogous to the seventeenth through nineteenth centuries in Europe—a time of volatile instability and political change. Moreover, Africa probably has a greater degree of ethnic, cultural, and linguistic pluralism than any other continent; so the process of nation making here is more complex and potentially more disruptive than elsewhere. Institutional breakdown, disorder, and political experimentation—all typical elements in the formative period of the nation-state—have been the dominant characteristics of the political process in much of Africa during the 1960s and 1970s and will continue to be so in the 1980s.

All these factors suggest that Africa is at a most difficult and explosive stage of development. During the 1980s quarrels within one country or between hostile neighboring countries are likely to erupt into violent conflicts, as they have often done since the European colonizers left, the efforts of the Organization of African Unity notwithstanding. Such conflicts will affect not only the localities or countries directly involved, but in many cases also will provoke foreign intervention. This is not to say that Africa will be the passive victim of international power politics. On the contrary, African factions will actively seek foreign military and economic assistance to bolster fragile positions, as they have frequently done already. Foreign powers, particularly the Soviet Union, will then intervene with little hesitation if they consider it in their best interests to do so. Although genuine détente between the United States and the Soviet Union would remove some of the powerful temptations to intervene that now exist—including certain Arab countries' desires to counter Soviet influence in the Horn of Africa—other temptations might continue to be equally attractive: competition for raw materials and Sino-Soviet rivalry. In short, the outlook for Africa in the 1980s is for continued internationalization of predictable local conflicts.

# ONE

# Fission and Fusion in Evolving Nation-States

## RENEWING LEGITIMACY

All African regimes are essentially temporary, or transitional, since with very few exceptions they do not operate within an established framework of viable and widely based institutions, even when they have been legitimatized. Even regimes that began with a high degree of legitimacy and popularity have tended to lose their popular base within short periods of from 5 to 10 years and as a result have often become coercive, thereby losing their claim to legitimacy. The successor regimes have had to start all over again to legitimatize themselves. This continuing process of "renewing legitimacy" is significantly different from the more familiar situation in world regions with well-established political institutions, in which power is transferred without major disruption. The disruption that historically has accompanied the transfer of power in new states is a crucial characteristic also of the contemporary period of Africa's political evolution.

## COMMUNAL POLITICS AND THE TRIBAL FACTOR

Africa's age-old communal conflicts were controlled, but not resolved, by the strongly centralized authority of each colonial power. A recrudescence of communal politics occurred during the period of anticolonial struggles and especially immediately after independence, when the power and authority of the successor regimes were mostly significantly weaker than those of the colonial rulers. This new and intensified phase of communal politics, which related primarily to the struggles for power in the newly independent states, contributed further to the weakening of governmental authority.

In a number of countries where strong ethnic communities felt the emergent nation-state to be a threat to their interests, the demand arose for new ethnic-states. It was in these situations that communal conflicts became most violent. Conflicts over the nation-state versus the ethnic-state are one major dimension of the postcolonial situation. However, it is unlikely (at least in the 1980s) that support for the *idea* of the nation-state will weaken, even though it is likely that a few ethnic-states might emerge. This prediction finds support in the experiences of both Nigeria and the Sudan, which retained their aspirations to become nation-states despite bitter civil wars related to demands for new ethnic-states. A different conclusion might be suggested by the experience of Ethiopia after the passing of Haile Selassie's era, but Ethiopia is sui generis, having emerged as an expanding imperial state more than 2,000 years ago.

The role of the "tribal factor" as a disruptive force weakening the effective authority of the evolving nation-state can be properly evaluated only by more rigorous classification of the different elements that are generally all lumped together under the generic of tribalism. There are four phases in the evolution of all nations: the period of clans, tribes, subnational (regional) groups, and national groups, or nations. Seldom is there a period in the enlargement of the "nation" when the earlier elements of clannishness, tribalism, or regional group interests cease to exist altogether.

*Clans* persist in many African countries as tightly integrated, small groupings of closely related family villages or nomadic communities. Although they speak the same language and share many common cultural traditions, they have not yet been integrated into a larger social and political organization with a more centralized authority. In the past, fierce loyalties resisted efforts to merge clans into a wider tribal, let alone national, loyalty;

intraclan tensions were prevalent, and clans cooperated (if at all) only when they felt their kinship clans to be actively threatened by some external force. The clan system of Scotland was a good example of what still persists in many parts of Africa. Even under the threat of English domination the Scottish clans did not all combine to resist the invader; some, in fact, allied themselves with the foreigner as a means of defending their own position against clan rivals (e.g., the ''black'' Campbells). A modern example of the clan system exists in Nigeria within the Ibo national group. Despite the modernizing process of Nigerian nationalism—and even though the impetus for this nationalism came largely from Ibo leaders themselves—clan feelings have survived to a considerable extent; their persistence was marked even during the war fought over the attempt to establish a Biafra Republic. In Somalia, on the other hand, modern nationalism has largely succeeded in producing a central focus of loyalty for the clans, but without altogether destroying fierce clan loyalties.

*Tribes* represent a higher political stage in the evolution of the clan system, with the tribal authority providing a more centralized power system. Although there are thousands of tribes throughout Africa, they are of varying size and internal cohesion, some numbering fewer than 100,000 and others totaling millions. Some of the larger tribes (such as the Ovambos of Namibia) exist within a loose system without an effective central authority; others (such as the Kikuyu of Kenya) still retain their separate clan loyalties but are capable of uniting behind a central leadership in times of crisis (as during the Mau Mau rebellion against the British), or to promote a collective tribal interest (as in their support for a Kikuyu-dominated government). But when it comes to the question of choosing a central leader, the intra-Kikuyu struggle can be fierce. This fact is illustrated by the prolonged dispute over a Kikuyu leader to succeed President Jomo Kenyatta, whose Kiambu clan insisted on nominating one of their number against claimants from other clans.

*Subnational groups* represent a further stage in the political unification process, by which time different tribes have achieved a level of integration and a common purpose within a large region. An interesting example of a subnational group is the Akans of

27

Ashanti and the affiliated Brong-Afaho peoples in Ghana. During the pre-Independence power struggle, when they felt their formerly dominant position threatened by Dr. Kwame Nkrumah's nationalist movement, the Convention People's party, they formed a powerful opposition centered on the old Ashanti Confederacy. Defeated in this struggle, they nevertheless persisted in their resistance and contributed largely to weakening Nkrumah's authority. President Nkrumah was ousted by a military coup in 1966, and the Akans succeeded in establishing themselves in a dominant position under Professor K. A. Busia's short-lived government of 1969–1972. One result of this latter development was to reactivate Ewe ethnic nationalism and irredentism, which has produced a strong demand for an Ewe ethnic-state.

*National groups* represent the final stage of the integration of the clans, tribes, and subnational groups into distinctive nations. In terms of numbers, territory, and common culture unity, they qualify in most respects for the status of nationhood.

These important distinctions become clearer if one examines the present situation in Nigeria. There one finds small communities that still cling tenaciously to their premodern clan system; tribes that resist becoming integrated into subnational groups; and national groups, such as the Hausa Fulani (numbering perhaps 20 million), the Yorubas (numbering about 12 million), and the Ibos (about 8 million). The clans and tribes see themselves as minorities defending their separate interests against the dominant national groups while at the same time engaging in local rivalries for power and influence in their own area. For their part, national entities have sought in the past to dominate the minorities living in their midst while also engaging in raw competition for central power with each other. Only if one sees the reality of Nigeria as a complex multinational state including a considerable number of minorities is it possible to evaluate the difficulties the country has experienced since its independence in evolving a workable federal constitution. Although Nigeria is perhaps an extreme example of communal problems in a single African country, it nevertheless provides a useful perspective for the complexities of virtually every other country on the continent.

## THE ROLE OF THE MODERNIZING ELITES IN THE EVOLUTION OF NATION-STATES

The modernization process in Africa has been, and will continue to be, the major factor in transforming narrow loyalties and interests into the wider loyalties required for the fulfillment of the nation-state. The impetus for national integration has come from the modernizing elites who emerged out of the colonial period as the dominant political force in every country in Africa (with perhaps the single exception of Swaziland). Nowhere has there been any serious ideological challenge to the aspiration of producing modern nation-states. The only such conflicts over this issue—and they have been very few—have been over claims that additional nation-states should be created by changing the borders existing at the time of independence in order to accommodate the demands of some militant ethnic groups to have a country of their own. However, despite fairly general acceptance of the idea of national integration, the concrete problems of achieving it—creating viable institutions and new value systems that can win the loyalty and cooperation of individuals and groups and can function without more institutionalized violence than the majority will accept—are formidable.

The present phase of the political process has three principal objectives: national integration, economic development, and defense of the new state from threats of internal and external attacks. Part of the third objective (internal order) is related to the success of the first two; another part (freedom from external attacks) is related to many points that are discussed later in this paper, such as the role of the Organization of African Unity (OAU), types of conflicts between neighboring countries, and internationalization of African conflicts.

The first two objectives—national integration and economic growth—are closely linked, since both are intended to promote a sense of shared national interest. Success or failure in achieving economic growth must be measured not only by the *degree* of growth but also by the fairness with which its fruits are distributed: greater wealth and new opportunities for higher education and better employment (especially the more highly rewarded and

29

prestigious jobs). If the priorities of development and social mobility favor a particular community, region, or economic-interest group to the neglect (or *felt* neglect) of others—as is frequently the case—communal tensions grow sharper, even though overall economic growth may be positive. In situations of sluggish economic growth, whenever the modernizers promise social and economic gains that cannot quickly be fulfilled, communal tensions likewise increase. Because the authority of the new state is mostly too weak to cope effectively with these tensions, the new rulers are often driven to defend themselves by resorting to force in varying degrees.

The process of nation-making is invariably accompanied by another destabilizing force: raw power struggles among competing pressure groups (often communal or regional in character) striving for control of the political machine, for a greater share of economic rewards, for status, and for privilege. These rivalries sometimes occur between new interest groups or classes, between established and ambitious ethnic communities, or between new challengers and those wishing to defend a previous dominant position in a particular area. Such conflicts often assume a communal or regional character because the natural political constituency in Africa is mainly the tribe or region—just as in the comparable period of American history the constituency was the state, region, or ethnic group.

Nevertheless, it is superficial and often misleading to use the phrase "intertribal rivalries" in describing the African political process during the formative period of the nation-state. It is misleading because the tribal factor is only one element in a complex struggle for power among competing pressure groups or even classes. Many of the more energetic and advanced tribes (which are obviously those most actively engaged in politics) are themselves made up of competing interest groups. This situation is the inevitable consequence of the modernizing process, which creates new economic and social-class interests. A proper analysis of the developing pattern of African politics demands that attention be paid to its horizontal (transtribal) as well as perpendicular (tribal) dimensions. Marxists will tend to place a greater emphasis on the inevitable growth of the class struggle, but even in the stage preceding class formation one sees the development of alliances consisting of special groups or sectional interests. One obvious reason for this is that since there are few countries in which a single tribe is able to dominate all the others, political alliances spring up among competing groups of tribes; this transtribal development is part of the growth of national politics. There is also the growth of new interest groups within a tribe that form alliances with similar interest groups in other tribes.

Two examples should suffice to show why it is misleading to speak too exclusively in terms of "tribal politics." In Kenya, the policies of Jomo Kenyatta succeeded in making the Kikuyu the dominant "tribal force." Yet in the succession struggle, the divisions have been just as marked between the different Kikuyu clans and economic-interest groups as between the Kikuyu and other tribes. Some of the Kikuyu aspirants to the presidency have found it necessary to enlist the support of non-Kikuyu, just as some non-Kikuyu aspirants have sought, and found, support among the Kikuyu themselves. Thus one sees the emergence of a new political system that blurs the narrowly exclusive Kikuyu-domination patterns established by Kenyatta.

The other example is provided by the political struggle among the emerging Zimbabwe political leaders of present-day Rhodesia. The usual portrayal of this stage of Zimbabwe politics is that there is a conflict between the two major tribes, the Shonas and the Ndebele. Yet the bitter internecine struggles inside the Zimbabwe Independence Liberation Army are largely among the Shona clans themselves; even these clan distinctions are not rigid but often overlap. Moreover, two of the leading contestants for power—Bishop Abel Muzorewa and Joshua Nkomo—enjoy the support of significant elements from among both the larger tribal groups. A more sophisticated analysis of the political situation would avoid some of the grosser errors made in describing developments too exclusively as "tribal." The tribe is undoubtedly important in determining the importance of a politician's constituency, but in and of itself it is not sufficient to sustain his or her power.

Nationalism and tribalism are conflicting forces; this, too, is one of the realities of the contemporary political process. To ignore this is to miss a vital element (in some countries already *the* vital element) of what might be anticipated in the 1980s. African politics are much less one-dimensional than misinformed Westerners realize, due, in general, to inaccurate portrayals in the Western mass media.

## VIOLENT COMMUNAL CONFLICTS

The struggle for power can turn violent when opposition groups feel a strong sense of exclusion from the political system, a deep fear of domination by a major communal group, and bitter grievances about regional neglect. Violence is likely to occur when such groups consider themselves strong enough to resist—and even more likely when they feel they can attract external support. However, a conciliatory approach by the threatened power center can soften opposition and bring the emergent nation-state a stage closer to becoming a reality.

In the Sudan, for example, the Negroid southerners—who converted to Christianity rather than to Islam during the colonial period when they gave up their animist beliefs—turned in 1956 to violence that lasted for about 15 years and produced strong secessionist aspirations in their region. They felt after the country's independence that they had no proper place in the new political system, which they alleged was totally dominated by the "Arab Muslim northerners." As a result of their struggle, the southerners achieved an acceptable federal constitution, although they were never completely unified during the "war for liberation of the south" and intracommunity rivalries still persist in the area. (Although all the communities are Nilotic, they do not have close tribal ties; the dominant Dinka group itself is fragmented into an active clan system.) What is remarkable, however, is the degree to which the southerners have developed a new focus of loyalty to the formerly hostile capital of Khartoum since President Gaafar al-Nimeiry, reversing his predecessors' policies, adopted a conciliatory approach toward them.

This transformation of loyalty was demonstrated in 1975 when the southerners backed the Khartoum regime against another armed uprising, this time coming from a dissident movement of Muslim northerners in the Western Region. Their rebellion grew essentially out of long-standing grievances about the neglect of development, education, and health facilities in their area, but was seized upon by Nimeiry's opponents in an effort to stage a military coup.

In both these examples of community conflict in the Sudan, the rebel forces obtained external support. The southerners were able to make use of kinship affinities in the neighboring countries of Ethiopia, Uganda, and Zaire to find refuge and maintain their clandestine organizations; they also received help from Israel because of Sudanese hostility to the Jewish state; and they had moral and some economic support from Christian churches in Europe. In the case of the rebellion in the Western Region, large-scale support came from neighboring Libya, whose leadership is hostile to the Sudan's, whereas friendly Egypt gave backing to Nimeiry in putting down this rebellion.

Parallels to the Sudanese situation are to be found in another spectacular example of communal conflict: the civil war in Nigeria (1967–1970) fought over the Ibos' attempt to secede and establish their predominantly ethnic state of Biafra. This conflict developed out of a power struggle between the mostly Christian Ibos, the Muslim Hausas, and the Christian and Muslim Yorubas that ended in a serious setback to Ibo ambitions. The Ibos feared domination from the Hausas of the northern states, a fear that turned to hatred and secessionism after a massacre of Ibos living in the north. On their side, the northerners had felt themselves to be threatened by Ibo economic and political domination. The third national group, the Yorubas, sided with the Hausas (though opposed to their political leadership) once the Ibos had proclaimed their ethnic-state. It is interesting to reflect that the Ibo leaders, who had felt driven to secession, were themselves the founders of Nigeria's modern nationalism, while the strongest feelings favoring ethnic-states originally came from the Hausas and the Yorubas. Yet faced with the possible breakup of the Nigerian state, it was these two forces that combined against the secessionists.

It is perhaps a significant pointer to the future that both the Nigerian and Sudanese civil wars, sanguinary as they were, ended with constitutional settlements that checked the development toward secession, at least for the present.

Another, much nastier, example of violent communal conflict (not yet fully resolved) is provided by the "double genocide" of the Hutus and the Tutsis, which began in 1958 when the numerically predominant Hutus in Rwanda (then still under Belgian rule) revolted against the minority Tutsi overlordship. A similar Tutsi overlordship existed in the neighboring Kingdom of Burundi, except that its system had allowed its Hutu minority a greater degree of upward social and political mobility than had been the experience of the Hutu majority in Rwanda. This unequal relationship in both countries, originally based on a bondage system, had persisted for centuries despite a long period of colonial rule by the Germans and Belgians, neither of whom had made any real attempt to change fundamental injustices. With the advance of the modernization process and the approach of political independence, the Hutus rose to liberate themselves. They succeeded in Rwanda after cruelly killing thousands of Tutsis and driving most of the survivors into Burundi. These events in Rwanda predictably turned the Tutsis of Burundi into strong defenders of their ancient position of privilege and their threatened security. In reaction to three separate attempts by the Hutus in the last 15 years to repeat their success of Rwanda in Burundi, the Tutsis have behaved with equal ferocity. Both sides have been guilty of great atrocities in this communal conflict, and the situation in Burundi remains dangerously unresolved.

Another unresolved communal conflict (though much less awesome than Burundi's) is to be found in Chad, where patterns of ethnic and geographical dominance are the exact reverse of those that sparked rebellion in the neighboring Sudan. At independence the majority Negroid southerners, mainly Christians and animists, dominated the central institutions and the ruling party; they concentrated economic and social development in their own region to the neglect of the pathetically undeveloped northern areas, which are mainly inhabited by Muslim clans and tribes.

Several rebel movements grew up in the north, of which the strongest was the Front for the National Liberation of Chad (FROLINAT). Like the Eritrean secessionists in Ethiopia, they initially sought to exploit the idea of an "oppressed Muslim minority" to win Arab support. Libya was quick to oblige, and the French responded by giving strong military support to the Chad government. After more than a decade of armed struggle, which has progressively eroded the authority of the center, the rebellion persists. But contrary to the other conflict situations already referred to, FROLINAT has not raised the demand of secessionism; this is mainly, but not exclusively, because its leadership is composed of modernizing nationalists. The situation has been further complicated by Libya's exploiting its support for FROLINAT to seize a substantial part of Chadian territory (see page 43).

## HUMAN RIGHTS IN THE NEW STATES

Throughout history the formative period of the nation-state has witnessed two conflicting developments: the expansion of some areas of freedom (e.g., greater social mobility, easier access to the sources of power, and wider economic and educational opportunities) and the curtailment of others (especially freedom of the press, the right to fair trials, and unfettered political activity). At the same time it must be remembered that many of these latter freedoms did not exist previously, and certainly not in Africa under colonial rule.

Postcolonial independence here has not ushered in a new era of liberty. However, notwithstanding the curtailment of some political rights, vastly greater numbers of people have become involved in the decision-making process—even in the single-party state systems—than was ever the case under colonial rule.

There are remarkably few—possibly no more than half a dozen—truly "closed societies" in independent Africa, e.g., Equatorial Guinea, the Republic of Guinea, the Central African Empire, Idi Amin's Uganda, and Muammar el-Qaddafi's Libya. While the majority of states can by no means be described as "open societies" in Western terms, most of them vibrate with political activity and open dissent. The dynamic interplay of political forces and ideas, the frequent challenges to authority and defiance of unpopular laws and leaders, all contribute to the essential political instability that, as has been pointed out, is the dominant reality of present-day Africa.

It is possible to take either a pessimistic or an optimistic view about the growth of liberty in Africa in the years ahead, since there is no possible way of evaluating the likely direction of change. Those who adopt a negative view about the chances of Africans ever governing themselves efficiently and fairly will obviously see the future in dark terms, but there is no objective reason for supposing that the human spirit that successfully transformed Western European nation-states into their present open societies, and is struggling today to achieve a similar transformation in Eastern Europe, will fail to assert itself any less tenaciously in Africa and in other parts of the Third World. The aspirations of Africans to be free (not just free of alien rule) are no different from those of Europeans or Americans. Only racists will, a priori, take an opposite view. The growth of democracy will assuredly be as unequal in Africa as it has been in Europe, with some societies developing the habit of democracy more quickly than others and with some, perhaps, becoming diverted into totalitarian states.

It is important to recognize that postimperial Africa is passing through a historic phase—and to remember that history cannot be measured in terms of single decades. The greatest cause for optimism is that the aspirations of the African modernizing elites are toward participatory democracy, however imperfect their practices in dealing with the immense difficulties they face.

# TWO

# The Role of the OAU in Dealing with Violent Conflicts

There are five principal reasons why the first pancontinental movement in history, the OAU, should have arisen in Africa. First, Africa was the only continent to remain almost entirely under colonial rule until the middle of the twentieth century; this meant that it was led into independence by modern-minded elites who shared a common experience of colonialism and similar educational backgrounds. Second, the element of "blackness" gave a continental dimension to the anticolonial struggle in Africa—and indeed inspired a much wider alliance among the world's "bottom dogs," mostly colored peoples. This sense of black unity had been fed since the late nineteenth century by pan-Africanist ideas and emotions originating largely in the black *galuth*. Third, the OAU represented a practical response to the balkanized condition of Africa at the end of its colonial experience, when the leaders of independent governments inherited many sensitive border problems caused by the artificially drawn frontiers imposed during the nineteenth-century "scramble for Africa"; there was thus a real need for an organization capable of stabilizing the new continental political system. Fourth, the nationalist elites understood that political cooperation was the best hope of developing modern economies and preventing their continent from continuing to be an area primarily for raw material exploitation. Thus the OAU initiated regional and functional organizations under continental supervision, such as the African Development Bank, the Trans-Africa Highway Commission, the

Inter-African Coffee Organization, and more than 40 other trading, banking, communications, and training bodies, which are also linked to the United Nations Economic Commission for Africa (ECA). Finally, the creators of the OAU shared a common purpose in wishing to ensure throughout the continent the completion of decolonization, which came to be known as the Unfinished Revolution; and its toughest challenge would come from the white-ruled parts of southern Africa.

The OAU, however, has suffered since its inception from the limitations inherent in all international organizations not dominated by a strong central power. They can be effective only when dealing with issues on which there is a general consensus. Attempts to impose the will of a simple majority would threaten the future of the organization, and since the preservation of unity is itself perceived as being vitally important, it follows that the OAU's ability to intervene in conflicts among its own members, or within any one of its member states, is strictly limited.

Members of the OAU are not bound to carry out decisions taken by its supreme body, the annual summit meeting of heads of state. The decisions of this body have the status only of recommendations, as in the case of the UN General Assembly. However, when a particular recommendation has the support of more than two-thirds of the OAU members, the dissenting minority finds itself under severe constraints not to act in open defiance of the great majority. One of the seven principles of the OAU enjoins noninterference by members in each other's internal affairs. While this principle has frequently been breached (as shown by the examples of intervention already mentioned), it has nevertheless served as a deterrent. What is more important, it has given victims of outside intervention a strong case with which to appeal to the OAU; its role in this respect has frequently been strongly on the side of the complainant.

Another of the OAU's principles binds all its members to recognize the borders existing at the time of independence and to avoid violent changes of boundaries. Machinery exists to bring about border rectifications through negotiation, mediation, and conciliation. Considering the potentialities for border conflicts, there were in fact relatively few during the 1960s and early 1970s.

Most of the border disputes (as between Upper Volta and Mali, Tanzania and Malawi, Nigeria and Cameroon) were either settled without force or, if not finally settled, kept simmering at a non-violent level through OAU diplomacy. Even in the very few instances when border conflicts did produce armed hostilities (as between Algeria and Morocco over the delineation of their Sahara frontier, or in the early conflict between Ethiopia and Somalia over the Ogaden in 1960) the fighting was quickly halted by OAU mediation. Nevertheless, irredentism remains a potentially disruptive force, as in the case of Ghana and Togo over the Ewe demand for "reunification," but especially over the aspirations for a Greater Somalia. (The violent conflict in the Ogaden in 1977 is discussed below.)

The OAU's capacity for crisis management has been tested most severely not only in the border disputes that have turned violent when sufficiently exacerbated by expansionist nationalism, but also in three other types of conflict: civil wars, disputes in which at least one of the superpowers has had a strong interest, and transborder armed subversion. Since these situations are likely to increase in the 1980s, there are reasons for particular concern about the OAU's future role as an effective regional organization in cases of violent conflicts.

## EXAMPLES OF FOUR TYPES OF VIOLENT CONFLICT

### Civil Wars

The OAU's principle of noninterference in members' internal affairs does not say that member states should refrain from taking sides in civil war situations but that their support should automatically go to the member government. (Thus in the civil war in Nigeria, when the Ibos attempted to set up their separatist Biafra Republic, the OAU members were expected to give their full backing to the federal cause.) Although half a dozen member states did in fact support the Biafrans (but without recognizing their Republic), the OAU's active role was to rally support for the Federal Military Government. Such a position robbed the

OAU of any effective role as mediator. Similarly, the OAU was completely paralyzed during the various outbreaks of Hutu-Tutsi genocide in Burundi. The Angola situation was different in that the civil war broke out at a time when there was still no recognized government. The OAU therefore took a firm stand in support of equal recognition for all three factions engaged in the power struggle; considerably more than two-thirds of the OAU members held to this line until the character of the civil war was transformed through external intervention, notably by the Soviets and Cuba taking the side of the Popular Movement for the Liberation of Angola (MPLA) and by South Africa and some Western nations backing the National Union for the Total Independence of Angola (UNITA) and the National Front for the Liberation of Angola (FNLA). Mainly because of South Africa's intervention against the MPLA, a two-thirds majority evolved in the OAU in favor of recognizing the MPLA.

### Expansionist Nationalism

Two key examples illustrate this particular problem in its African context. The first is the pan-Somali ambitions of the Somali Democratic Republic, which seeks to change both territorial borders and the political system in northeast Africa. Since two of Somalia's neighbors, Ethiopia and Kenya, are also members of the OAU, the Organization has been inhibited from taking sides. However, it has been able to keep alive its role as mediator, and was successful in preventing the conflict from becoming openly violent for many years, until the character of events changed in the Horn of Africa because of the disintegrating power of the Ethiopian regime.

The second example is provided by the conflict over the former Spanish Sahara. Morocco and Mauritania made an agreement with Spain in 1976 whereby the territory was divided between them, and thus their frontiers were considerably enlarged. Algeria, for reasons of national interest and a coincident interest in seeking to defend the principle of national self-determination, took the side of the majority of the inhabitants of the Spanish Sahara, who violently resisted the attempt to incorporate them into Morocco and Mauritania. Sufficient OAU member states supported Algeria's position to prevent outright African recognition of the Moroccan and Mauritanian claims, but these were not enough to secure recognition for the Sahara Arab Democratic Republic proclaimed by the Saharans. The result was a bitter desert war and a debilitating crisis within the OAU itself over this question.

### Foreign Intervention in African Conflicts

Although the OAU is firmly opposed to any external interference in the continent's internal conflicts, it has not had much success in preventing "foreign meddling." For example, Ethiopia was unsuccessful in getting support to dissuade a number of Arab states as well as Soviet-bloc countries from openly supporting the Eritrean secessionist struggle. Since practically all the OAU members are opposed to secession of any kind, they had every reason for responding positively to the Ethiopians' appeal. Nevertheless the OAU showed itself incapable of mobilizing its members to make a strong demarche against countries such as Syria, Iraq, and Saudi Arabia, which provided most of the economic and military aid needed to sustain the Eritrean liberation movement. In the case of the civil war in Angola, the course of events was decided in the end not by the OAU but by the forces of external intervention.

Clearly, therefore, the OAU has so far not had much success in implementing its policy of resisting foreign intervention in essentially African disputes. There is little reason to suppose that the Organization will be able to act any more effectively in defense of its principle of nonintervention by foreign powers in the 1980s.

### Transborder Military Intervention

There are already signs that a much more dangerous level of external intervention is likely to threaten the African political system in the 1980s unless the OAU is able to develop a greater capacity to enforce its authority over its member states in defense of its charter. This new threat, which can be characterized as "military coups by proxy," is the result of three developments in the present African political system. First, the growth of single-party states or military regimes means that an opposition, no matter how large, can seldom hope to win power by peaceful methods. Second, the increasing armed strength of African countries means that a coup can succeed usually only by the use of force. The third development is the growth of hostile neighbor states. This set of circumstances provides the basis for an alliance between a dissident movement in a particular country and a neighboring regime that shares an interest in overthrowing that country's government. There is a growing list of examples to support the view that this is not just a passing phenomenon but one that, unless it can be checked, may establish a new pattern of military conflict on the continent.

In September 1973, Tanzania allowed the forces of the ousted Ugandan President, Milton Obote, to be mobilized on its territory for a military invasion across its border to topple the usurper, President Idi Amin. Because this action was seen by many as a legitimate attempt by the legal President of Uganda to unmake the coup that had toppled him and because of the distaste for Amin, this form of intervention by President Julius Nyerere's regime was regarded in some quarters as having been justified. However, the failure of the countercoup seriously embarrassed the Tanzanians.

President Qaddafi of Libya is perhaps the leading exponent of the tactic of the proxy military coup. In 1976 he helped to arm and train one of the Sudan's opposition movements to enable it to stage a military invasion across the Libyan frontier which only narrowly failed. Qaddafi's interest in this enterprise was his bitter hostility to President Nimeiry of the Sudan, a close ally of Egypt's President Anwar el-Sadat, another of Qaddafi's enemies. This pattern was soon afterward repeated in Ethiopia, whose military regime, the Dergue, is also hostile to Nimeiry because of his supposed support for the regime's opponents. The Dergue therefore became an ally of Qaddafi; together they encouraged a fresh regrouping of Sudanese opposition forces in Ethiopia to prepare for a further attempt to unseat the regime in Khartoum. Reacting to these moves, the Sudan invoked the military support of Egypt, thereby escalating the confrontation among the four African neighbors.

The Libyan leader has also provided military support for the rebels in Chad. Qaddafi's interest in intervening in Chad was twofold: to help the Muslim minority obtain a larger share in the government of Chad and to get a government sympathetic to his claim for border changes, which would enable Libya to obtain an area reputedly rich in minerals. Libya also occupied an area of its other neighbor, Niger, and has had a hand in the conflicts between its military leaders.

The so-called Katangese invasions of Zaire across the Angola border early in 1977 and 1978 are other examples of transborder aggression. After the MPLA's victory in Angola in 1976, President Mobutu Sese Seko of Zaire continued to support its opponents by backing a plan to send a military force of dissident Angolans and mercenaries into Angola's oil-rich enclave of Cabinda. When this plan was discovered, the Angola regime allowed—probably even encouraged—the Front for the National Liberation of the Congo to invade the Shaba (Katanga) province of Zaire. This invasion was represented at the time as either an attempt by the former Katangese Gendarmerie to fulfill the late Moise Tshombe's ambition of bringing about the secession of Katanga or as a further thrust by the Angolan Marxist regime, with Russian and Cuban backing, to expand its influence in Zaire. In fact, when seen in an African context, this conflict was essentially between two hostile neighboring regimes, each wishing to overthrow the other and each using the opposition forces of its neighbor to legitimatize its own intervention. It should be noted, however, that there was also external intervention by Morocco and France, who came to Zaire's support.

These few glaring examples of the emerging pattern of the proxy military coup illustrate the serious dangers in the growing phenomenon of military coups being supported by outsiders who give military and economic aid to opposition movements that, by themselves, would be too weak to mount an effective challenge against their own regimes.

# THREE

# International Dimensions of Violent Communal Conflict

## ESCALATION OF LOCAL CONFLICTS

There are three levels of violent communal conflict: territorial, regional, and international.

*Territorial violence* is confined within the borders of a single country and does not involve external forces to any significant degree. Regional violence occurs when communal conflict spreads beyond the borders of a single country as a result of neighboring countries taking active sides in the conflict. So far, neighboring countries have not used their own armies in support of rival communal causes. However, as mentioned earlier, Algeria has intervened in the Western (formerly Spanish) Sahara in support of the Polisario Front against Morocco and Mauritania. The Soviet Union supports Algeria's stand in this conflict, while Spain and France support the two latter countries. For the most part, when a neighboring country has become engaged on one side of a communal struggle, it has done so—as previously discussed—by supplying arms to the rebels and by allowing them to organize their resistance from bases in its territory.

*Regional violence* has occurred in four different types of situations in Africa: first, when a state has feared that its own national interests, especially its security, might be threatened by the outcome of a serious internal conflict in a neighboring country; second, when strong hostile neighboring regimes have sought to subvert and overthrow each other by clandestinely supporting communal groups that, for their own particular reasons, have wished to change the regime in their own country; third, when a regime has supported an antigovernment force in a neighboring state as a means of exerting leverage on its neighbor; fourth, though only very rarely, when issues of unalloyed principle have been involved.

The most dramatic example of the first kind of situation was the major intervention by the Zaire government in Angola, particularly after the collapse of Portuguese colonialism in early 1974. President Mobutu's regime saw the emergence of a neighboring regime headed by the MPLA as a threat to his own government. He feared that its pronounced Marxist leanings would impact strongly on the internal politics of Zaire, and he also feared the expansion of Russian influence in the area, especially since Moscow supports a number of Mobutu's political opponents. For these reasons Mobutu strongly supported the MPLA's two rival movements, the FNLA and UNITA, both of whom drew their support primarily from ethnic communities. Because the Mobutu regime decided to treat the conflict in Angola as a question affecting Zaire's national interest, it not only intervened itself but also urged first the People's Republic of China and later the United States, France, and eventually South Africa to intervene. It is doubtful whether the Angolan civil war would have reached the level of international involvement it did had it not been for Zaire's role; its successful appeal for support of the FNLA and UNITA was a major reason why the MPLA asked for and got such large-scale military aid from Russia and Cuba. The Russians also happened to see their own national interests involved, since they did not want movements endorsed by the Chinese emerging victoriously in Angola—quite apart from their obvious wish to eliminate Western influence wherever possible.

The best known example of the second kind of situation, the proxy military coup, is the Somali Republic's long-standing conflict with Ethiopia. Also, Libya has on several occasions attempted to subvert and overthrow its neighboring regimes: President Sadat's in Egypt, President Nimeiry's in the Sudan, President Habib Bourguiba's in Tunisia, and President N'Garta Tombalbaye's (as well as, later, President Félix Malloum's) in Chad.

There are many instances of the third type of situation, in which an opposition movement has been used as a means of exerting leverage on a neighboring regime. One particularly interesting example was Emperor Haile Selassie's manipulation of the southern Sudanese rebel movement to get the Sudan regime to stop supporting the Eritrean rebels in his own country. Support for the southern Sudanese was turned on or off depending entirely on the current policies pursued by the Khartoum regime toward Eritrea. Successive Egyptian regimes have not infrequently used this type of leverage.

Two rare examples of support being given to a challenging movement purely for reasons of principle both involve Tanzania. During the civil war in Nigeria, President Nyerere openly declared himself on the side of the Biafra Republic because he felt the Ibos were justified in demanding secession. He also allowed his country to become involved in the conflict in Uganda—to the point of allowing the ousted President Milton Obote to launch a military attack from Tanzania's soil—primarily because of his loathing for General Idi Amin's murderous policies.

However, the outstanding example of support being given to challenging communal groups for reasons of principle is the stand taken by the African states in the conflicts over Rhodesia, South Africa, Namibia, and at an earlier date, the Portuguese colonies. The potentials for international conflict arising from the struggles for black majority rule in southern Africa are discussed later.

*International involvement* in regional conflicts has taken the form of direct or proxy involvement by major powers, to which reference has already been made. Sometimes this involvement can be more or less forced on one or the other of the major powers if one of their specially favored regimes is acting to further its own national interests in a cause that may not necessarily be of any interest to the foreign ally itself.

These elements of international involvement in what are essentially regional conflicts are of a different order from situations in which major powers become involved primarily because of their own interests and which produce a different magnitude of international violence. Such situations (e.g., that in Angola) produce the greatest dangers for international intervention; they are considered separately below.

## REASONS FOR INTERNATIONAL INVOLVEMENT

In the 1950s and 1960s the major Western powers and the Soviet bloc intervened actively in situations from which they hoped to be able to produce regimes friendly to themselves. However, in the latter part of the 1970s, the Western powers began to show themselves to be much less ready to become directly involved in local power struggles, while the Soviets became more adventurous, e.g., in Amin's Uganda, in the Horn of Africa, in Libya, and in southern Africa. Unless there is a major reversal of this trend in Western policies in the 1980s, initiatives for outside intervention are much more likely to come from the Soviets, with the Chinese and some of the Western nations possibly reacting to their moves in particular circumstances. It seems unlikely, though, that the United States or the West European nations will, as in the past, be ready to rush forward in support of a particularly friendly African regime under threat from some "Marxist" challenger (as in the case of President Mobutu in Zaire) or to give clandestine support to pro-Western political opposition movements (as with Holden Roberto's FNLA in Angola). What is more clearly in the cards is that Western nations will react in support of groups of African states through open agreements in defense of shared interests.

A significant new development in the late 1970s was the emergence of militantly anti-Soviet groups of African and Arab states, which for their own reasons wish to resist what they regard as spreading Soviet influence on the continent. This development was paralleled by the emergence of several Marxist-Leninist regimes, as in Angola and Mozambique, which, though not showing any wish to become part of the Soviet bloc, might increasingly come to see Cuba as a model for a new alliance of revolutionary regimes within the Third World. Such a grouping would, like Cuba, derive most of its support from the Soviets. Although there are likely to be more of these two different types of regimes in the 1980s, the majority of African states, whether militantly left-wing (e.g., Algeria, Tanzania, and Madagascar) or radically nationalistic (e.g., Nigeria and Ghana), are nevertheless likely to cling determinedly to their aspirations for nonalignment. All these developments will, predictably, be heavily influenced by what happens in the Middle East and in southern Africa. (These situations are discussed below.)

These predictions need to be heavily qualified by continuous reminders of the transitory nature of virtually all the present regimes in Africa—as indeed of most regimes throughout the Third World. There is no certainty whatsoever that any of the present leaders will survive the decade of the 1980s. Usually a change of leader brings with it a change of regime, and quite often, too, a radical change in the country's international orientation. Thus countries such as, say, Egypt or the Sudan, which now identify more strongly with the West than with the Soviets, could revert to their earlier anti-Western positions. *This fluidity in Third World political directions is likely to remain a dominant reality in future international relations.*

Five issues are likely to keep Africa high on the agenda of international decision making in the 1980s:

1. "Ocean politics," a crucial aspect of the global power struggle
2. The racial confrontation in Southern Africa, which will almost certainly reach its climax before the end of the next decade
3. Afro-Arab politics
4. Sino-Soviet rivalry for influence in the Third World
5. The North-South dialogue over a "New International Economic Order"

The first four issues are discussed below; the fifth is discussed in the other studies in this volume.

### Ocean Politics

The emergence of the Soviet Union as a world naval power for the first time in its history has created new strategic interests for Moscow in obtaining naval facilities in all the major oceans. Moscow has three objectives: first, to be capable of effective defensive reaction to any new threat of strategic superiority by the Western alliance; second, to develop its ocean and air supply routes around, and across, the African continent from the Indian to the Atlantic oceans as well as to develop its communication lines through the Red Sea to the Indian subcontinent in order to contain what Moscow sees as a deadly threat from China; third, to enlarge the Soviet sphere of political and economic influence. The strategy of the architect of the modern Russian Navy, Admiral of the Fleet Sergei Gorshkov, calls for naval facilities right around the coasts of Africa; these can be assured only through the establishment of friendly littoral states along the Red Sea, the Mediterranean, and the Indian and Atlantic oceans. There are strong forces opposed to the ideas embodied in the Gorshkov strategy.

The Western powers are not alone in wishing to deny "military bases" to the Russians. The majority of African nations, because of their policies of nonalignment, are eager to deny bases to any of the major powers. The Chinese, with no present interest in acquiring foreign military positions of their own, have strong reasons for allying themselves with the Third World in opposing military bases for any of the superpowers. A group of Arab countries—led by Saudi Arabia, Egypt, and the Sudan (also backed by Iran)—all strongly oppose the granting of special naval facilities to the Russians.

The first phase of the struggle over the role of the Russian Navy in the Red Sea will have been largely decided by the beginning of the 1980s since the present conflicts in the Horn of Africa will by then presumably have reached some conclusion. But whatever new balance of power is struck in the Horn, the strategic importance of the Red Sea and the surrounding waterways will continue to attract considerable foreign interest.

Three other areas of major interest for Russian strategists are southern Africa, the West African "bulge" on the Atlantic, and the southern littoral of the Mediterranean. It would require nothing short of a major reversal of Gorshkov's strategy for the Soviets to lose interest in any of these areas—but it is by no means clear just how heavy a political and economic commitment Moscow is ready to make to secure military facilities around the coasts of Africa. However, the importance Moscow gives to this aspect of its policy is verified by the bold and imaginative gamble it took in the Horn of Africa in the 1960s and 1970s.

In pursuit of Gorshkov's strategy, the Russians agreed in the early 1960s to train and equip the Somali Army in exchange for obtaining naval facilities at Berbera on the Red Sea. However, their greater interest has always been with Somalia's hostile neighbor, Ethiopia, whose strategic advantages in Africa are far greater than anything Somalia could provide. In 1959 the Russians had offered to help train and equip the Emperor's Army, but their offer was rejected in favor of more substantial aid from the United States, with whose policies the Emperor was in any event more sympathetic. Having been rejected by the Ethiopians, Moscow settled for Somalia as second best. But after the Emperor's downfall in 1974, the Russians resumed their interest in Ethiopia. Their problem, then, was how to court the new military regime in Addis Ababa without alienating the Somalis at a time when the latter were in a stronger position than ever before to press their claims for reshaping their borders in the Ogaden province as well as to extend their effective influence over Djibouti. The Somalis naturally feared that if Soviet arms were to be used to strengthen the Ethiopians, their national ambitions would be harder, if not impossible, to achieve. The Soviets sought to reassure the Somalis by proposing that if United States influence could be removed from the area, Moscow would be in a strong position to mediate between the neighbors and to assist in the process of border changes—especially since the French were planning to withdraw from Djibouti. The plan amounted to nothing less than the establishment of a *Pax Sovietica* over the Horn of Africa. Despite strong Somali opposition, Moscow pressed ahead with its design, even though doing this meant risking the loss of what it had already gained in Somalia. It is not yet possible to write the end of this particular chapter in the development of the Soviets' strategy, but their high-risk policy in the area shows the high priority they give to expanding their influence over the Red Sea littoral states.

## Racial Confrontation in Southern Africa

The most difficult and critical decisions that will have to be taken in Africa in the 1980s will almost certainly be settled before the end of the decade. It is difficult to see how the communal and

51

other types of conflict in this important region—especially in the Republic of South Africa—can be resolved without violence or without international involvement. What is less easy to predict is the scale of violence that will occur during the transformation of white power in the subcontinent and the nature of world intervention. The major Western powers have already begun to orient their policies away from the white communities in the region toward support for black majority rule—a shift of interest proclaimed by Dr. Henry Kissinger, when still U.S. Secretary of State, in his major policy statement in Lusaka in April 1976. This Western shift of policy makes it less likely that the major powers will find themselves on opposite sides of the mainly racial barricades south of the Zambesi River, but it by no means rules out the possibility that they will find themselves supporting rival causes during the critical period of the breakup of the present political system in South Africa. Western policies will almost certainly be more ambiguous than those of the Soviets or the Chinese because of old economic and ethnic-historic relations with South Africa. If Western policies should appear to Africans to be supportive of white South Africans or "moderate" blacks, there would be a strong possibility of an angry anti-Western reaction, not just in the subcontinent itself but right across Africa and into the Third World. Such a reaction would obviously favor a much greater role for the Soviets and/or the Chinese in the predictably dramatic last chapter of white dominance on the continent.

## Afro-Arab Politics

Arab involvement in Africa grew significantly in the decade of the 1970s for a number of different reasons, the major ones being the greater support given by black African governments to the Arab states for the restoration of the territories occupied by Israel after the Six Day War in 1967 and, especially, their sympathy for the Palestinians' cause. The outflow of the Middle Eastern crisis is therefore bound to condition both Afro-Arab and Afro-Western relations.

Until the diplomatic rupture between African states and Israel over the October 1973 War, the consistent position of the great majority of the OAU members was to back UN decisions on the Middle East, recognize Israel's right to exist, and support a separate Palestinian state. Since the 1973 watershed, black African states can be expected overwhelmingly to take the Arabs'side in crisis situations, but in times of low tension they will give strong support to mediation efforts for a negotiated settlement along the lines of UN Resolutions 242 and 338. African support for the controversial UN General Assembly resolution equating Zionism with racism should be viewed as a position useful for diplomatic trade-offs between black Africans and Arabs rather than an expression of genuine conviction.

Afro-Arab relations are by no means smooth. One serious cause of tension is the effect on most of the African economies of the quadrupling of fuel costs. Although the Arab League provided funds to compensate African countries worst hit by the higher fuel costs, the size of these funds and the controversies surrounding their creation produced strains in Afro-Arab relations that still persist. Another major cause of tension has been the involvement by virtually all the Middle Eastern states in the conflicts in the Horn of Africa on the side of the Somalis and the Eritreans. Arab support for both these causes was at first justified on the ground of helping Muslim communities to achieve justice. At the same time, a number of Arab states and the Sudan have pursued an activist role in the area in reaction to the greater Russian involvement in the Red Sea. (See "Ocean Politics" above.) Arab support for supposedly Muslim causes in Africa has been carried furthest by Libya's President Qaddafi. Whenever he has intervened anywhere on the continent, he has made no attempt to disguise his major interest in promoting the cause of Islam. On the contrary, this is a major element in his revolutionary ideology. The Libyan leader's intervention on the side of Uganda's President Amin (backed also by the Palestinians) is likely to leave a bitter legacy of conflict between Muslim and Christian Ugandans.

The greater wealth of the oil-producing Arab states and the increased role of the Arabs in the OAU have produced in the minds of some black African countries a sense of Arab "manipulation" or "domination." But these difficulties should not be exaggerated, especially since the Arabs do not operate as a bloc. Inter-Arab rivalries (as between Libya/Egypt and Sudan, or Libya/Tunisia and Morocco) are likely to be more disruptive than Afro-Arab tensions.

## Sino-Soviet Rivalries in Africa

The obsessional rivalry between Moscow and Peking over their fears about each other's world hegemonic ambitions is likely to become an even more critical factor in the politics of the Third World in the 1980s than it already showed signs of becoming in the previous decade.[1] In their global confrontation, the Russians and the Chinese both pursue a major foreign policy interest in seeking to counteract each other's influence. This rivalry was an important determinant in the Russian decision to intervene in Angola and Uganda, and it is a major element in Moscow's foreign policy in Mozambique. The Chinese have played an active role in giving support to governments or liberation movements that are hostile to Moscow. This tendency by the Chinese and Russians to give their support to rival leaders and movements is well suited to widening communal and other conflicts in African countries, since schismatic movements can hope to attract support from one or the other of the communist world centers if they declare themselves to be on one side or the other in the Sino-Soviet rivalry for influence in the Third World. Thus, for example, the Russians worked actively to persuade the South-West African People's Organization of Namibia (SWAPO) to phase out its Chinese support in exchange for greater Soviet aid. In the Rhodesia (Zimbabwe) conflict, the Russians have backed the Zimbabwe African People's Union (ZAPU) led by Joshua Nkomo because the Zimbabwe African National Union (ZANU) forces have looked to the Chinese for their military training. At a different level, when the Nimeiry regime in the Sudan broke

[1]The rivalries between the two international communist capitals are considered more fully in another 1980s Project study. See Alan S. Whiting and Robert F. Dernberger, *China's Future*, McGraw-Hill for the Council on Foreign Relations, New York, 1977.

its military ties with the Russians in the early 1970s, the Chinese agreed to supply it with urgently needed light military equipment, and when the Russians refused to supply spare parts for Egypt's MIG aircraft, the Chinese agreed to do so.

In the developing crises in southern Africa and elsewhere on the continent, there is every reason to suppose that Sino-Soviet rivalry will be at least as important an element in foreign intervention as Soviet-Western rivalry—assuming, of course, that there is no rapprochement between Peking and Moscow.

## PATTERNS OF INTERNATIONAL INVOLVEMENT

One of the mythologies of contemporary Africa is that the continent is the victim of exploiting foreign powers. But an objective analysis will show that this belief is a postcolonial hangover from the days when Africa was indeed the passive victim of the major powers. The situation today is that foreign intervention occurs because African governments, individually or collectively, for their own interests, are ready to engage external support; when these local interests happen to suit a particular foreign interest, the risk arises that a purely internal conflict will become internationalized. One such example was the deliberate initiative of Zaire and of two of the Angolan liberation movements it supported to enlist the aid of the United States, France, and South Africa in the Angolan conflict. Their initiative was matched by the MPLA and its African supporters in encouraging and endorsing the intervention of the U.S.S.R. and the Cubans. Another example is the interest of a number of Francophone African states, such as the Ivory Coast, Senegal, and Gabon, in retaining the economic and military support of France. A different kind of example was the willingness of the OAU Liberation Committee to accept and encourage foreign military and economic support for the liberation movements of southern Africa; as it turned out, only the Soviets and the Chinese were willing, for their own interests, to respond to this African initiative.

Reference has already been made to the way in which Somalia introduced the Russian presence into the Red Sea area for its own national interests, only to find later that the Russians were more interested in building on the Somali bridgehead an edifice from which they could extend their influence throughout the Horn of Africa. A common feature of this type of foreign involvement is the wish of African governments—especially those that come to power through coups—to attract the support of a strong foreign ally to provide them with the economic, technical, and military support they need to defend their newly acquired power. Past experience shows no clear pattern of the effects of a reorientation of foreign policy on domestic policies. On the whole, capitalist-minded or non-Marxist socialist governments prefer to seek Western support precisely because they do not want their policies or societies to be unduly influenced by communist ideas. On the other hand, the few revolutionary-type regimes (Angola, Mozambique, Guinea, the People's Republic of the Congo, and Somalia) avidly seek out Western or "capitalist" Arab economic support, but without substantially altering their domestic policies. In situations where Soviet or Chinese aid has not been effective in developing local resources (e.g., uranium and other mining enterprises in Guinea) or when communist technology is behind that of the West (e.g., offshore oil drilling in Angola), Marxist-minded regimes are pragmatic enough to adapt their policies to accommodate foreign investors in a private sector of their economies. Only one African country—Somalia—has in the past changed its political system after orienting its foreign policy toward Moscow and Peking. While there is, predictably, a greater input of either Western or communist ideas into the political systems of countries oriented strongly toward one or another of the world centers, it is difficult to extrapolate from previous events the likely effects in the 1980s of changes in foreign orientation on the domestic policies of African countries.

However, there is one important area of change in the African political process resulting from changes in foreign policy: when a regime pitches itself strongly toward the West, the Soviets, or Peking, the opposition will generally go in the other direction. This appears to be one of the dialectics in the continent's domestic policies, and there is no reason to believe this will not continue into the 1980s. The usual pattern is that when a "pro-Western" government has been overthrown, the new regime invites the support of an "anti-Western" power. Thus when the Sudanese leader, General Nimeiry, first took power with his Revolutionary Command Council in 1970, he denounced the West and declared himself strongly on the side of the "progressive bloc of nations led by the Soviet Union." The Russians, pursuing their interests in the Horn of Africa, responded enthusiastically by providing substantial military support and promising economic aid. However, a few years later, when Nimeiry found himself engaged in putting down a communist-supported coup, he expelled the Russians and sought military aid from the Chinese. When this aid proved inadequate, especially after the deepening crisis in the Horn of Africa and the Red Sea area, Nimeiry turned to the conservative Arab states (notably Saudi Arabia) and to the West. They, for their own interests, replaced the Russian presence in the Sudan. Thus, within a period of five years, the Sudan's foreign policy orientation underwent a 180-degree change.

At least a score of similar examples could help to illustrate the thesis that foreign involvement is as much a product of African politics as of foreign interests. Predictably, so long as African governments need to buttress their power by enlisting foreign alliances and so long as the major powers (or even middle-level powers—such as France, Yugoslavia, Israel, Iran, and the major Arab states) conceive it to be in their interest to support particular governments, the process of internationalization will continue. It is doubtful whether Africa can ever really isolate itself from the currents of world politics.

What, then, of the OAU's aspirations to nonalignment? Nonalignment does not mean, as is commonly and wrongly supposed, that its practitioners should desist from having links with any of the major powers. It only requires of them that they should not take sides automatically in the conflicts between the major military blocs or offer them military bases. Nevertheless, there is sometimes a contradiction between the aspirations and practice of nonalignment that derives from the policies of the major powers themselves, since they often withhold their support from those countries that might appear to be oriented toward either the East or the West. If Western-Soviet or Sino-Soviet global strategic and economic rivalries should cease to be as competitive as they have been up to the present, it will become easier for those wishing to be truly nonaligned to achieve their aspirations. Meanwhile, in countries where none of the major powers has a particular economic or strategic interest it is already possible for their governments to receive aid from all the competing world powers.

This analysis leads to the conclusion that a major by-product of successful détente between the West and the Soviets will be a lessening of foreign involvement in Africa, although competition for easy access to strategic raw materials might become more important in the future. However, even a lessening of Western-Soviet tensions would still leave the problems of intervention that derive from Sino-Soviet rivalry. Will the West be uninterested in the outcome of the competition for influence between Moscow and Peking? This is a major issue that is still too little discussed, but it lies outside the scope of this study.

# FOUR

# Mapping Potential Conflicts

Virtually every important African country is capable of reproducing the conditions of serious violence and international involvement witnessed in the Nigerian civil war in the late 1960s and in Angola in the 1970s, in the rebellions in the Sudan, Eritrea, and Chad, and in the postindependence power struggle in the former Belgian Congo (now Zaire). Reasons for offering such a prognosis have already been broadly indicated but may be briefly recapitulated:

- The continent is in a state of flux, as more than 50 new nations-in-the-making are engaged in the difficult task of trying to create viable institutions that will achieve political and economic equilibrium for their pluralistic societies.

- When these attempts fail completely, the outcome is either a military regime (which is never stable), an authoritarian regime (e.g., that of Kwame Nkrumah in Ghana, Sékou Touré in Guinea, or more extremely, Idi Amin in Uganda and Macie Nguema Biyogo in Equatorial Guinea), or a period of widespread disorder.

- Serious breakdowns in the evolutionary process invariably result in violence or even, in certain circumstances, in civil war. An additional source of instability and conflict comes from national rivalries between neighboring states. Examples of this are Somalia/Ethiopia/Kenya, Zaire/Angola, Algeria/

Morocco/Mauritania, Libya/Egypt/Sudan, and Uganda/Tanzania/Kenya.

- Rival forces in local power struggles use the opportunities available to them in the international community to seek foreign support in order to strengthen their own side; this situation can lead to the internationalization of local disputes in particular conflicts, depending on how the various major powers, or some middle powers, perceive their national or ideological interests (e.g., the Arabs in Eritrea or the Russians, Americans, Chinese, and South Africans in Angola). A checklist of countries or regions that under certain circumstances could produce situations involving large-scale violence and possible external intervention would include the following:

*Southern Africa.* The region lying roughly south of the Zambesi River will unquestionably be the most dangerous part of the continent in the 1980s. Its conflicts are essentially communal in origin, since they arise from the powerful wish of the African majorities of Rhodesia, Namibia, and the Republic of South Africa to play a dominant role in the political systems of their countries and the equally powerful determination of the white minorities (especially the 4 million in South Africa) to defend their way of life and protect their future security. The situation is already heavily internationalized, partly because of considerable Western economic investments there, as well as the conceived Western interest in the strategic importance of the Cape of Good Hope sea route and Western desire for continued access to the abundant strategic mineral resources of the area; and partly because of the role of the Soviets, the Chinese, and the Third World countries in the developing conflicts. It is safe to assume that by the early 1980s Rhodesia (renamed Zimbabwe) and possibly also Namibia (formerly South-West Africa) will have achieved their independence as African majority-ruled states. It is more difficult to predict whether the final denouement of the independence struggle will result in anti-Western governments in those two countries. But what seems certain is that "white" South Africa will find itself in a state of isolation on the continent and probably also in a state of siege, with its fate likely to be settled before the end of the 1980s. Clearly, therefore, the decade will see southern Africa figuring high on the list of foreign policy priorities of all the major world powers as well as many of the smaller powers—and of course it will be a top priority for the nations of Africa.

*Nigeria.* The continent's most populous country, now on its way to becoming one of its richest, has in the past failed to maintain institutions capable of keeping the balance between its three major national groups (Hausa-Fulani, Yoruba, and Ibo) as well as between them and the substantial minority groups in the country. Although the civil war did not leave any lasting wounds, it is still a reminder of what could again happen in the future. Nigeria is a turbulent, assertive country with deep cleavages. The experience of the recent civil war suggests that foreign powers will be prepared to take sides in the event of the recurrence of a serious civil conflict. The rapid growth of oil wealth could contribute to further instability unless it is equitably distributed. By the early 1980s the country will have embarked on an important new federal constitutional experiment whose success or failure will be of decisive importance.

*Zaire and Angola.* Although General Mobutu has established a vigorous personal authoritarian regime, Zaire's position in the region has become vulnerable since the emergence of the Marxist MPLA regime in Angola (with strong Russian and Cuban backing). Zaire's immediate northern neighbor, the People's Republic of the Congo, enjoys military support from the communist nations as well as economic support from France. The Russians' and Cubans' successful intervention on behalf of the MPLA has already encouraged Mobutu's adversaries to seek to overthrow him by enlisting support for their cause (see the section on transborder conflicts). A new situation would be created in the region if Angola, Zaire, and the Congo were all to come under the rule of Marxist-type regimes. If these regimes were in harmony with each other, the challenge to other less radical governments in the area would produce one kind of crisis; but if, as is not unlikely, their different national interests were to drive the military radicals into sharper confrontation with each other, the risks of major

61

international involvement would become greater. There is also the strong possibility that the communal conflicts within Angola will continue, and so long as the MPLA regime relies so heavily for its security on the Cubans and Russians it is predictable that the opposition elements, especially among the Ovimbundu peoples in the south, will seek to attract the support of South Africa and of anticommunist elements in the Western community.

*The Horn of Africa.* A period of historic change in the power structure of the Red Sea region began after the passing of Emperor Haile Selassie's rule in the mid-1970s. The stability of the Horn for centuries had rested largely on the "Christian Highlands" of Ethiopia, whose control was buttressed in more recent times by French control of Djibouti. Ethiopia's back door through the Sudan was secured by a neighborly interest in maintaining the region's stability. Western influence was predominant in the area, and the Arab world showed relatively little interest in the affairs of the African coast of the Red Sea before 1960. This long-established power system was finally shattered by five rapid developments. First, with the disintegration of imperial power came a decline in Ethiopia's military effectiveness and the release of age-old fissiparous forces throughout the ancient empire. Second, Somalia emerged to independence in 1960, with expanding nationalist ambitions and with links to the Muslim world. Third, the Soviets, pursuing the strategic interests made possible by their new Navy, embarked on an activist role in the Red Sea area as a major supplier of arms. Fourth, the French colonial period was ending in Djibouti. Fifth, the neighboring Arab states, together with the Sudan, became actively involved in the struggles in and around the Horn.

While some kind of resolution to the immediate conflicts in the area might be expected to occur by the end of the 1970s, it would be surprising if the rivalry for power and influence within this strategic corner of the continent were not to continue to invite the active interest of foreign powers in the next decade.

*East Africa.* The death of President Jomo Kenyatta in 1978 left Kenya without a really effective successor capable of maintaining the kind of stability known under his rule. By the early 1980s the country's politics will, predictably, be turbulent, and its effects could be felt throughout the region.

By the 1980s the situation in Uganda is likely to have undergone major changes. Although it is not possible to offer any firm predictions about the nature of these changes, two alternatives present themselves. The first is that a post-Amin regime may be headed by a cadre of radical young military officers who swing their power to Russian military support for at least the initial period of their new regime. Such a regime would obviously produce a new situation in East Africa. An alternative possibility is that the post-Amin regime will consist of a coalition of forces representing disaffected regions in Uganda that have developed strong grievances against the role of the Nubians and Muslims during the Amin period, as well as against the Arab states (especially Libya) and the Soviets. There could be a period of bitter vengeance. By the 1980s, too, President Julius Nyerere's dominant leadership will have run its course in Tanzania if he sticks to his present intentions of retiring at the end of his current tenure.

The probability is that throughout East Africa the 1980s will be a time of considerable change and possibly considerable instability. East Africa's problems will also be considerably influenced by developments in the two neighboring regions: the Horn of Africa and southern Africa.

*The Sudan.* While the country has recovered remarkably from the long civil war between the north and south, the southerners' confidence in constitutional guarantees still depends very largely on the personal survival of General Nimeiry as President. If he should be replaced—and he is constantly under threat—the Sudan could again become seriously divided; but next time the south would find itself in a much stronger position to maintain its stand, since it has already acquired its own regional government and a regionally based trained military force. If Nimeiry were to be replaced by another northern leader capable of quickly engaging the southerners' trust, no great damage would be done. But if the new regime were to be formed either by the old sectarian religious leaders or, worse still, by the challenging Muslim Brothers (the Islamic Charter Front), the dangers of a new period of violent communal politics could not be ruled out. Russia is the principal major power recently involved in Sudanese conflicts. The Egyptians, the Saudi Arabians, and the Libyans have been closely concerned with the country's politics, the first two on opposite sides from the last. Ethiopia, Uganda, and Zaire are other neighbors most likely to be affected by any fresh upheavals in the Sudan.

*The Maghreb.* Of all the regions on the continent, the northwestern Mediterranean littoral states have moved toward becoming viable nation-states. It is still too early, though, to conclude that there will be no major upsets in this area.

The rule of King Hassan II of Morocco is still largely personal. The stability of Algeria's political system has been strengthened under Colonel Houari Boumedienne's leadership, but communal and regional tensions (especially in the Kabyle) persist. The Maghreb's maverick, Libya's Colonel Qaddafi, has so far failed to wield any real influence on the region other than to serve as a goad to his neighbors. However, his ideas about a revolutionary Islamic revival make some appeal to opposition groups in the Arab world, and his dedicated commitment to Palestinian militancy wins him admirers. But he has also so far failed to develop any important base of support outside Libya. If Qaddafi should survive into the 1980s and learn from his many past mistakes, his role could acquire a greater importance in the next decade.

Despite many encouraging signs, the Maghreb remains an area of potential trouble. The military confrontations between Algeria and Morocco—first over their unsettled boundaries and more recently over the Western Sahara—are a reminder of how brittle the relationships remain between these powerfully armed neighbors. While the Maghreb nations maintain close economic links with Western Europe, Algeria and Libya have at the same time developed new ties with the Russians.

*The End of the Era of the Septuagenarians.* A number of African countries owe their present relative stability to the leadership of the men who brought them to independence. A common feature of their rule is that they have not prepared the way for a smooth succession, succeeded in creating durable institutions, or advanced the development of national integration. In a number of countries the present leaders are closely identified with particular tribal, regional, or other sectional interests. The succession struggle after they leave the scene is bound to be a time of political instability and uncertainty in their countries in the 1980s, and because such struggles involve the mobilization of community and regional support behind "favorite sons," it is possible to foresee a period of greatly sharpened communal tensions.

This description applies to Guinea (President Sékou Touré), Malawi (President Hastings Kamuzu Banda), the Ivory Coast (President Félix Houphouët-Boigny), Senegal (President Léopold Senghor), and, to a much smaller degree, Tunisia (President Habib Bourguiba).

## CONCLUSIONS

Africa's postcolonial conditions of political instability will, if anything, be greater in the 1980s than in the two previous decades. The struggles to achieve internal equilibrium within the continent's multiethnic evolving nation-states and to construct a continental security system are likely to elude early solutions, and will in all probability produce recurrent breakdowns within the 50-odd countries involved as well as precipitate damaging conflicts between states. The alarming increase of more sophisticated weapons on the continent and the greater national expenditures on armaments will intensify the scale of violence of such conflicts. At the same time, the deepening economic crises facing most African countries will contribute to continental and governmental instability as well as strain the relations between African countries and, especially, the Western industrial nations. The climacteric of the racial confrontation in southern Africa during the coming decade could seriously impair Afro-Western relations.

The African continent will not remain isolated from the conflicts in the rest of the world community, notwithstanding the pan-Africanist aspiration toward nonalignment. Only the achievement of genuine détente between the West and the Soviet bloc will lessen the interests of the major powers in the continent, but the persistence of Sino-Soviet rivalry would be a continuing disturbing factor in Africa's political instability.

So long as there are important powers—the Soviets, China, the West, and the Arabs—ready to provide economic and military support for African rival governments or movements, a strong incentive will remain for these rivals to present their causes in ways most likely to attract the kind of external support they need to achieve their aims. In this way local conflicts will continue to attract external intervention, and they will, on occasion, produce conflicts of a major international character.

Even if the major Western powers should wish to disengage from an interventionist role in Africa, it is hard to see how their global interests will allow this to happen so long as the Soviets, at least, remain unwilling to match such a Western disengagement.

In brief, issues related to Africa are likely to engage a great deal of international attention in the 1980s.

# Social and Political Trends in Africa in the 1980s

I. William Zartman

# Introduction

Africa has thus far fared rather poorly at the hands of those who would tell its future. The earliest prophet of the continent noted the impossibility of his task in a single sentence: "*Ex Africa semper aliquid novi*" ("Something new is always coming from Africa"), said Pliny the Elder, in wonder. Bertrand de Jouvenal's pioneering *Futuribles* (1963) was foresighted enough to include a long chapter on Africa, by René Servoise; it has proven quite correct in its economic part (which is, in fact, similar to the economic basis of this present chapter) and totally wrong in its political part (which concentrates on single parties and African unity). Finally, the ultimate critique of predictive methodology, *Long-Term Projections of Power*, written in 1973 by Oskar Morgenstern, Klaus Heiss, and Klaus Knorr, makes one mention of Africa in the 1980s and in it speaks of "the Portuguese colonies." We can do no worse here.

The following discussion singles out four elements that are central to sociopolitical trends within the continent and to African relations with non-African countries during the next 15 years: natural resources, generational succession, subregional configurations, and external penetration. To begin with a discussion of resource base may seem to imply that politics is subservient to economics. Although the answer is partly a matter of defi-

NOTE: I am most grateful for the time and comments of Philip Allen, David Hapgood, Stephen Low, and Timothy Shaw, which have been helpful in preparing this paper.

nition, no such subservience is intended here. If the standard Parsonian definition of politics as "the authoritative allocation of values" is adopted, politics can be seen to be very much related to the amounts of such values that are available for allocation. There may be many ways of accomplishing such allocation, but it is the resource base that defines those possibilities, particularly in a middle-range projection of a decade and a half.

Of course, resources are not merely finite material endowments, such as oil deposits. Also included are more flexible material aggregates that can be generated as well as distributed, such as gross national product (GNP), and even intangible components, such as organized skills and mobilized energies. Politics is the business of generation and distribution, organization and mobilization; it is intimately, even inextricably, connected with economics; they are two sides of the same societal coin, and as in the case of a two-sided coin, it is impossible to say that one is any more dependent on the other than the reverse.

Resources are already scarce or underutilized throughout most of Africa, and the tension between population growth and resources, particularly food, may be expected to produce conflicts that seem to be ethnic or class-based but are fundamentally economic. The present disparity between African countries that are relatively well off and those that are less so will increase. The poorer countries will frequently have authoritarian governments that concentrate on maintaining order and keeping the lid on demands for improved conditions, whereas richer countries will probably continue to expand under governments led by a new generation of civilians who are pragmatic about problems of development and political competition.

Only a handful of countries—Algeria and Nigeria and perhaps Morocco and Zaire—will have sufficient resources and sufficient efficiency in exploiting them to qualify as contenders in a struggle for continental leadership and Third World influence. But continental appeals for action will, in any case, be of less interest to Africans than cooperation (or conflict) within geographical subregions. As they draw more closely inward upon themselves, the subregions will not be greatly concerned with ideology, except in southern Africa, where the struggle against white-minority governments will intensify.

Throughout Africa, foreign influence is predicted to diminish, as indigenous life-styles, products, and solutions to problems are increasingly desired. Foreign investment will certainly not disappear, but increasingly it will be conducted on African terms. The few remaining foreign troops will most likely be withdrawn from the continent during the 1980s, a return to colonialism is almost unthinkable, and the creation of puppet governments by foreign states is equally unlikely.

In contrast to the old days of bilateral dependence on a colonial country, in the future sovereign African states will tend to diversify their foreign relationships. At the continental level, African states striving for leadership will probably espouse militant policies toward the North for their own political ends; the geographical subregions will tend to be more moderate. It is only at the latter level that African groupings will be able to deal effectively with the North—not only because of the relatively pragmatic policies likely to be followed within subregional groups, but also because here, rather than at the continental level, will be found a solidarity of socioeconomic and hence political interests that makes real negotiations with outsiders possible.

How confident are these predictions for the 1980s? It is hard to be sure, partly because of the explosive potential of southern Africa and the uncertain evolution of détente between the United States and the Soviet Union. If the independence of Zimbabwe (as Rhodesia will be called) is achieved relatively quickly by a negotiated settlement, this should make it easier for fundamental changes to occur peacefully in the Republic of South Africa. But if bitter guerrilla fighting continues in Zimbabwe too long, nationalist movements will become even more radicalized; all-out war may break out; and states throughout the world are likely to become deeply involved in the conflict. In this case, the South African situation will overshadow everything else, and economic growth and cooperation within Africa—as well as fruitful relationships with the North—will suffer greatly.

71

To take account of these alternative predictions, the latter part of this paper presents two "scenarios": one "uneventful" and relatively optimistic, the other "eventful" and pessimistic. It is unlikely that the history of the 1980s will closely follow either scenario, but it does appear likely that it will incorporate events from both in some proportion, probably shifting back and forth from one to the other.

# ONE

# Trends

## RESOURCES AND LEADERSHIP STRUGGLES

Before discussing more concretely the resources and politics of Africa, it may be useful to define a government system generally as an entity that receives supports and demands from its people and combines them to produce supplies and controls. In brief, *supports* include expressions of patriotism and allegiance; the goods and services produced by citizens' labor; the taxes this productivity generates; and citizen participation in such government enterprises as the civil service, elections, the military, or a jury system. *Demands* by citizens comprise their expectations concerning a great variety of services related to, for example, law and order, defense, employment, health, social change, housing, education, and transportation, and their distribution. *Supplies* may include government-financed projects; assistance to private business and industry; and innumerable types of help to individuals, from job-training programs to distribution of welfare; as well as less tangible activities, such as researching problems of development, setting national priorities, and soliciting foreign aid and investment. *Controls* exerted by government may include allocation of scarce material resources; policies to regulate prices, wages, money supply, and other aspects of the financial system; maintenance by the police of law and order; and so on.

The more complex the society, the more diverse will be its supports, demands, supplies, and controls; but the supports and supplies always comprise in large part the resources of the society, and demands directly concern the way in which resources are allocated. The balance among these components creates the context for different political strategies. For example, when demands are stronger than supports, the state must increase either controls (to dampen demands) or supplies (to raise supports), and when demands outrun supplies, either supports or controls must be increased. This is not the place for a conceptual treatise, but it is important to specify the relation between policy and resources.

In the 1980s and beyond, balances between resources and burdens in African nations will be affected by the evolution in the size and structure of their populations, changes that will create difficulties for governments as they seek to sustain or achieve sound rates of economic growth. A medium-variant projection from 1970 by the UN forecasts a 75 percent increase in the African population by the end of the 1980s and a doubled population in 25 years, as the result of an annual growth rate of about 2.75 percent.[1] Generally, the largest countries have the largest rate of increase: most of the states with an annual population growth rate greater than 3 percent are among the 10 most populous mainland African states (11 if Egypt is included), and the rest are scattered about. (The top 10 are, in order, Nigeria, Ethiopia, Zaire, South Africa, Sudan, Morocco, Algeria, Tanzania, Kenya, and Uganda.)These states are not necessarily the richest, however. None except Algeria, Morocco, and South Africa among the top 10 had a per capita GNP exceeding $300 in 1975, and none but Algeria, Morocco, South Africa, and Nigeria will have one exceeding $350 in 1980 or 1985. Nor are economic potentials improving rapidly. Of the 7 states with a per capita GNP growth rate exceeding 4 percent during 1965–1975, only Nigeria, an oil state, is from among the top 10 most populous ones, and the rest—Guinea-Bissau, Gabon, Swaziland, Botswana, Libya, Tunisia—are smaller. On the other end of the spectrum, approximately half the African states had a per capita

---

[1]Medium-variant, or "most plausible," projection from UN, Department of Economic and Social Affairs, Population Division, *World Population Prospects as Assessed in 1973*, ST/ESA/SER.A/60 (New York, 1977), p. 90.

GNP growth rate of less than 2 percent during 1965–1975, and some of these (Zambia, the Sudan, Senegal, Niger, Equatorial Guinea, Upper Volta) had a zero or negative rate (see Table 1). Not even an effective population control program, in itself unlikely, could change this picture before 1980.

Instead, population structures are likely to aggravate rather than alleviate the burdens on African polities through the 1980s. Nearly half of the population is now and will continue to be in the dependent age sectors (under 15 years old or over 65), and this percentage may increase if the women giving birth to the doubling population stay at home with their babies. Such sectors are the heaviest users of schools, hospitals, and other social services, in addition to being economically unproductive. Yet, paradoxically, the labor force is even now threatened with unemployment and underemployment. There must be a commensurate increase in jobs to handle the 3 percent population increase and an additional increase—perhaps as high as twice the first figure—in urban employment to meet the 4 to 7 percent urban growth rate (compared with a rural growth rate of 1.5 to 3 percent). There must be investment of 12 percent of the national income (based on a standard 4:1 capital-output ratio) to maintain the standard of living for the increasing population and something like a doubling of this figure to increase living standards. Only the states that have the resources and have begun the growth to meet these rates in the past decade are likely to be able to do so in the coming one.

One other aspect of the population structure is more hopeful. Illiteracy is not likely to be eradicated by 1990 in any country, nor is complete primary education of the relevant age group likely to be achieved in many places, but a growing number of children will have passed through each level of education. The educated percentage of each age cohort will vary considerably, depending on the economic resources and educational policies of each country, but a growing modern sector of society will be available for productive employment and for certain political activities that are discussed more fully in the next section of this chapter.

So far, these projections for economic and population growth have assumed that African countries will change in the future at the same rate as they did in the past. How reasonable is it to

## TABLE 1
### Basic Data

| Country | Population 1975 (millions) | GNP 1975 ($ billions) | Per Capita GNP 1975 ($) | 1965–1975 growth rate, % | 1980 ($) | 1990 ($) | Military 1976 ($ thousands) | Education 1970 | 1980 (% of age group)* | Independence |
|---|---|---|---|---|---|---|---|---|---|---|
| Nigeria | 80.0 | 28.8" | 330 | 5.3 | 425 | 720 | 270' | 34- 4-0.3 | 60- 8-1 | 1960 |
| Egypt | 37.3 | 11.3 | 310 | 1.0 | 325 | 360 | 400.0 | 68-32-7.8 | 70-40-12 | 1922 |
| Ethiopia | 28.0 | 2.9 | 100 | 1.3 | 105 | 125 | 65' | 18- 4-0.2 | 25- 8-0.5 | † |
| Zaire | 24.9 | 5.5 | 220 | 2.0 | 245 | 300 | 55' | u-11-0.8 | u-15-1 | 1960 |
| South Africa | 24.5 | 29.2 | 1,200 | 2.0 | 1,920 | 3,000 | 109 | u-27-4.8 | u-40-6 | 1910 |
| Sudan | 17.8 | 2.8 | 150 | 0 | 150 | 150 | 50 | 33- 6-1.0 | 50-10-2 | 1956 |
| Morocco | 17.3 | 8.4 | 520 | 3.1 | 605 | 825 | 90 | 55-12-1.2 | 65-20-3 | 1956 |
| Algeria | 16.8 | 11.1" | 680 | 3.8 | 790 | 1,100 | 85 | 75-11-1.7 | u-20-3 | 1962 |
| Tanzania | 15.2 | 3.1 | 170 | 1.9 | 185 | 230 | 25 | 36- 3-0.2 | 55- 5-0.5 | 1961 |
| Kenya | 13.4 | 3.1 | 220 | 3.1 | 255 | 350 | 9 | 64- 9-1.0 | 85-15-2 | 1963 |
| Uganda | 11.6 | 3.4 | 250 | 0 | 250 | 260 | 25' | 50- 4-0.6 | 55-4-0.7 | 1962 |
| Ghana | 9.9 | 5.3 | 460 | 0.8 | 480 | 520 | 20' | 58- 9-0.7 | 60-12-1 | 1957 |
| Mozambique | 8.7 | 3.6 | 400 | 3.8 | 480 | 700 | 21 | 70- 9-0.5 | 75-10-0.5 | 1975 |
| Madagascar | 8.7 | 1.7 | 190 | 0.6 | 195 | 210 | 17' | 85-11-1.0 | u-12-1.5 | 1960 |

| | | | | | | | | | |
|---|---|---|---|---|---|---|---|---|---|
| *Cameroon* | 6.4 | 2.4 | 330 | 3.7 | 395 | <u>600</u> | 10 | u- 9-0.6 | u-15-1.5 | 1960 |
| *Zimbabwe* | 6.3 | 3.2 | 510 | 2.9 | 565 | <u>750</u> | 17 | u- 5-1.0 | u- 9-2 | 1978? |
| *Ivory Coast* | 6.2 | 3.6 | 500 | 3.9 | 605 | <u>890</u> | 8 | 75- 5-1.2 | u-20-2 | 1960 |
| <u>*Angola*</u> | 5.9 | 3.4" | 580 | 3.5 | 690 | <u>970</u> | 35 | 75- 9-0.5 | 85-12-0.5 | 1975 |
| *Upper Volta* | 5.9 | 0.6 | 100 | 0 | 100 | 100 | 10' | 13- 1-0.0 | 20- 1-0.3 | 1960 |
| *Mali* | 5.7 | 0.6 | 100 | 2.4 | 115 | 145 | 6' | 20- 3-0.1 | 30- 4-0.3 | 1960 |
| *Tunisia* | 5.7 | 4.4" | 760 | 5.8 | 1,000 | <u>1,770</u> | 21' | u-21-2.3 | u-30-4 | 1956 |
| *Guinea* | 5.5 | 0.7 | 130 | 1.1 | 135 | 140 | 10 | 33-13-0.6 | 35-10-1 | 1958 |
| *Malawi* | 5.0 | 0.8 | 150 | 3.5 | 175 | 250 | 4 | 50- 2-1.0 | 60- 5-1.5 | 1964 |
| *Zambia* | 4.9 | 2.7 | 340 | -0.5 | 330 | 350 | 17 | 80-12-1.0 | u-15-2 | 1964 |
| *Niger* | 4.6 | 0.6 | 130 | -3.0 | 130 | 130 | 4' | 14- 1-0.0 | 20- 2-0.3 | 1960 |
| *Senegal* | 4.2 | 2.0 | 370 | -0.4 | 370 | 370 | 11 | 43-10-0.5 | 60-15-1 | 1960 |
| *Rwanda* | 4.2 | 0.4 | 90 | 1.5 | 100 | 115 | 4' | 75- 2-0.2 | 70- 2-0.5 | 1962 |
| *Chad* | 4.0 | 0.5 | 120 | 1.4 | 130 | 150 | 11' | 30- 2-0.0 | 30- 2-0.1 | 1960 |
| *Burundi* | 3.8 | 0.4 | 100 | 1.3 | 105 | 115 | 7' | 28- 2-0.2 | 30- 2-0.1 | 1962 |
| *Somalia* | 3.2 | 0.3 | 100 | 1.0 | 105 | 115 | 31' | 10- 4-0.4 | 30-10-0.5 | 1960 |
| *Benin* | 3.1 | 0.4 | 140 | 0.5 | 145 | 165 | 3' | 40- 5-0.1 | 50- 5-1 | 1960 |
| *Sierra Leone* | 2.8 | 0.6 | 200 | 0.8 | 210 | 235 | 3 | 35- 9-0.5 | 40-10-1 | 1961 |
| <u>*Libya*</u> | 2.4 | 11.5" | 4,270 | 5.8 | 5,400 | <u>8,800</u> | 25' | u-22-3.4 | u-50-10 | 1951 |
| *Togo* | 2.2 | 0.6 | 270 | 1.5 | 290 | 335 | 4' | 75- 8-1.5 | u-12-1 | 1960 |
| *Cent. Afr. Emp.* | 1.8 | 0.5 | 230 | 0.6 | 235 | 250 | 4' | 73- 5-0.1 | 85- 9-1 | 1960 |

## TABLE 1 (Continued)

### Basic Data

| Country | Population 1975 (millions) | GNP 1975 ($ billions) | Per Capita GNP | | | | Military 1976 ($ thousands) | Education | | Independence |
| | | | 1975 ($) | 1965–1975 growth rate, % | 1980 ($) | 1990 ($) | | 1970 | 1980 | |
| | | | | | | | | (% of age group)* | | |
| Liberia | 1.7 | 0.7 | 410 | 2.1 | 450 | 540 | 6' | 43-12-1.1 | 70-20-2 | † |
| Congo Rep. | 1.4 | 0.7" | 500 | 2.6 | 570 | 735 | 10' | u-25-2.2 | u-60-5 | 1960 |
| Mauritania | 1.3 | 0.4 | 310 | 2.7 | 345 | 450 | 15' | 16- 3-? | 20- 5-0.5 | 1960 |
| Lesotho | 1.2 | 0.2 | 180 | 3.5 | 215 | 300 | 1 | 95- 7-0.5 | u-15-1 | 1966 |
| Namibia | 0.8 | 0.9 | 980 | 3.0 | 1,135 | 1,525 | 0 | na | na | 1978? |
| Botswana | 0.7 | 0.2 | 290 | 9.0 | 300 | 670 | 1 | 66- 8-0.3 | 80-15-1 | 1966 |
| Guinea-Bissau | 0.5 | 0.2 | 330 | 5.0 | 420 | 590 | 5 | 38- 6-0.0 | 75- 9-0.5 | 1973 |
| Gabon | 0.5 | 1.0" | 1,760 | 8.0 | 2,400 | 3,500 | 3 | u-16-0.4 | u-30-3 | 1960 |
| Swaziland | 0.5 | 0.2 | 420 | 6.0 | 560 | 1,000 | 2 | 84-17-0.4 | u-35-1 | 1968 |
| Gambia | 0.5 | 0.1 | 180 | 3.0 | 210 | 280 | 1 | 32- 9-0.0 | 40-15-0.5 | 1965 |
| Equat. Guinea | 0.3 | 0.1 | 260 | -1.0 | 250 | 250 | 5 | u-17-0.0 | u-20-0.0 | 1968 |
| Djibouti | 0.2 | 0.2 | 1,580 | 2.0 | 1,750 | 2,200 | 0 | na | na | 1977 |

SOURCES: UN, International Bank for Reconstruction and Development, UNESCO, U.S. Arms Control and Disarmament Agency, OECD.

78

*Figures refer to percentage of 6 to 12, 13 to 18, and 20- to 24-year-old groups in primary, secondary, and higher education.
'Indicates military regime.
"Indicates petroleum exporter.
ᵘIndicates universal primary education.
†Indicates not applicable.
<u>Richest</u> countries are solid underlined; poorer countries are dotted underlined. ┄┄┄┄
na = not available.

assume continuity in economic growth rates? In a few cases, new raw materials may be discovered. Some of the more advanced West African states, such as Senegal, Ghana, the Ivory Coast, or Cameroon, might improve their performance if they discover some offshore oil, as nearby Nigeria has already done. Raw materials in a number of other states may be depleted before the end of the century; Mauritanian iron is an example, and oil reserves in most producer states may be similarly affected. High energy prices may dampen some growth rates. A number of states with unusually high growth rates, such as Libya, Botswana, Swaziland, and Gabon, are unlikely to be able to keep up the pace, and by the same token the negative growth rates found in places such as Senegal and Niger are unlikely to continue until they become extinct. But in general, the African states that are now relatively rich compared with the poorer states on the continent are likely to remain so. A wise economic policy can certainly cause some important variations in these programmed destinies, and a wasteful policy can exhaust savings and resources. Yet, all in all, account taken for the limitations on exceptionally high and exceptionally low rates and room left for a realistic dose of human error and divine inspiration, growth rate continuity can give a sound basis for understanding the range of possibilities in the next 10 to 15 years.

Another aspect of the balance of burdens and resources is likely not to stay constant but to become worse, and this is Africa's ability to feed itself. Africa's per capita food production has remained constant over the past 20 years and in the next 15 years cannot be expected to increase as fast as population growth. Four aspects of this trend will be briefly noted; a full discussion of their causes is outside the scope of this chapter. First, traditional African agriculture is becoming increasingly incapable of feeding even the rural population, which, though occupying a declining proportion of the total, is nevertheless increasing with the rest. Second, modern agriculture is also lagging behind population growth, since the attraction of jobs and welfare policies in the towns, the difficulty of getting goods from producers to consumers, and the sparsity of farm credits and facilities all work to remove incentives from the primary sector. Africa can increase its agricultural productivity only with truly massive imports of capital (for seed and fertilizer, among other things) and technology—possible only through huge new aid programs. More likely is a large increase in cereal deficits, tripling in the poorer countries between 1975 and 1985 and increasing 25-fold in Nigeria in the same period. Third, where agriculture is favored, it is oriented to export crops that earn hard currency for urban commercial, administrative, and industrial growth. Fourth, in some areas—notably the Sahel of the Sahara—all these factors, aggravated by climatic conditions, serve to undermine the defense of marginally arable land against the desert. At present, sub-Saharan Africa is estimated to be cultivating only 27 percent of its 643 million hectares of land considered suitable for agriculture and producing less than 1 percent of its maximum agricultural production of $11,681 \times 10^8$ kilograms of consumable protein. Furthermore, it is estimated that ¼ million hectares are lost to the Sahara in an average year. Simple ecological defense is beyond the means of most affected states, and reclamation faster than the population growth rate is beyond the means of any of them.

Added together, these elements have immediate consequences. Governments either must make a major effort to change agricultural policies or depend on increasingly large food imports (either as purchased goods or as public aid) or face the basic problems of food shortages and unrest. Complacent governments have fallen over this problem in the 1970s in Ethiopia, Chad, Niger, and others and will do so in the 1980s as well. Food purchases, when they are possible, deplete scarce currency reserves even in the developing parts of the underdeveloped world; even if large aid programs were undertaken by the developed world, they would have other costs, including serious political problems of intervention and dependence. The first option—intensified agricultural production—is of course preferable as well as theoretically possible. Agricultural yields and acreage can be increased, so that continuing decline need not be the only basis of forecasts into the 1980s. But a policy of rapid agricultural growth requires capacities for control, mobilization, knowledge, and implementation, not to speak of pump-priming resources, that African states have not shown to date, with very few exceptions.

These trends indicate that Africa as a whole will continue to undergo a Malthusian crisis compounded by a distributional crisis. That is to say, population growth is likely to put increasingly heavy strains on already inadequate resources before it finally levels off and adequate productive capabilities are developed, probably around the turn of the millennium. This pressure will be compounded as national groups compete for the allocation and equitable distribution of scarce resources. Indeed, the recent evolution of Africa can be broadly encompassed in these same terms. Any other elements—such as ethnic rivalries or class conflicts—are merely second-level manifestations of the basic issue.

The postwar colonial years (1945–1960) were generally characterized by economic growth, but the main beneficiaries of this growth were the colonizing populations. This situation gave rise to nationalist movements as a protest against unequal distribution and to struggles for independence as a means of reallocating benefits to the national population. But in the subsequent 15 years (1960–1975), once independence was gained, growth was slow. Moreover, the redistributive aims of the nationalist movement created expectations that were too great for the meager resources of independent governments to meet. Where there have been enough supplies to meet demands, the small nationalist groups that came to power have remained and under the best of conditions have achieved some measure of economic, social, and political development. It is no accident that the original single-party elites tend to continue in power in the African states with the higher economic growth rates: Kenya, Cameroon, the Ivory Coast, Tunisia, Malawi, Gabon, omitting the recent oil states and recently liberated ones. More often, the original small group has been replaced by another—the military—who have acted forcefully to freeze demands. It is again no accident that military regimes frequently exist in countries with lower growth rates: the Sudan, Uganda, Upper Volta, Niger, Benin, the Central African Empire (CAE), Madagascar, and Ghana, among others.

These conditions remain the basic parameters of what can be

expected to happen in the 1980s. In those states where the supplies of resources can be increased, new demand managers will be able to take over under various forms of political competition; but where resources cannot be increased there will be less room for competition, order and the control of demands will become the first job of the government, and therefore pressure for the increase of supplies will be reduced. Thus richer developing countries will do better in seeking to expand their resources than will relatively poorer countries.

Redistributional measures usually inhibit growth in the short run, but if properly carried out can give it impetus in the longer reach. Energies can be released, competition can open up for new positions and opportunities, and a growing demand for goods and services can stimulate increased production. When redistribution takes place without sufficient resulting growth, there is endemic frustration and a sense of deprivation that can be met in various ways. A revolution of falling satisfactions can bring in new leadership, but it may again spend energies on new redistributions rather than new growth. To prevent such a revolution, incumbents can resort to increased controls if they cannot increase supplies. If no growth is possible to enable continued redistribution, demands on the government eventually must fall, although in the process they may be directed against outside sources, as blame, requests, or conditions. In any case, few of these eventualities are conducive to economic development or to its social and political analogs: mobility (social development) and institutionalized problem solving in which the citizenry participates (political development).

Realities of economic, social, and political development are not, however, as clearly correlated as some development indicators make it appear. African states will continue to be concentrated rather than egalitarian systems—ruled by, and to some extent for, sociopolitical minorities. Higher-income states, as pointed out earlier, are likely to be able to accommodate internal rivals for leadership, but the more numerous lower-income states are likely to undergo both intense struggles and sudden changes among the various ethnic and socioeconomic groups contending for the enjoyment of scarce goods.

By the 1980s some of the African states—the "developing" states—will be doing significantly better than the rest—the "underdeveloping" states—in their ability to control access to and use of their own resources. They will therefore be in a position to claim leadership and woo followers in continental affairs. The difference between the two groups is important and provides a more accurate picture than the generally described "widening development gap," which is true but only partially so. Algeria, Nigeria, and possibly Zaire and Morocco have a good chance of continuing development that sets them apart from others, with sizable GNP and a considerable economic weight that could provide the means and aspirations for leadership roles in Africa. Another group of states also has a high per capita GNP growth rate and is active in inter-African politics but is unlikely to have the weight and drive of the first group: Libya, the Ivory Coast, Tunisia, Cameroon, and, to a slightly lesser extent, Kenya, Malawi, Liberia, Botswana, and perhaps Zimbabwe. Angola and Mozambique also had a high per capita growth rate before independence and may have recovered it by the 1980s. Alongside of these, as can be seen in Table 1, are poor states with a per capita growth rate of about 1 percent or less: Burundi, the Central African Empire, Chad, Benin, Ethiopia, Guinea, Equatorial Guinea, Madagascar, Niger, Rwanda, Sierra Leone, Somalia, the Sudan, Togo, Uganda, Upper Volta. Another group of states has a relatively high per capita GNP (over $300) that is stagnating: Ghana, Senegal, Zambia, and currently Zimbabwe. Thus, as time goes on, African states will spread out more and more on the economic development spectrum. As this occurs, they will constitute stronger and weaker states, united by common concerns for resource generation but divided by the success of their responses to the problem.

Conflicts over resources within a particular country are inviting situations for external interference by those African states that are competing for leadership on the continental level. Furthermore, the distributional crisis in Africa will provide an issue on which aspiring continental leaders can try to lead other African and like-minded Third World states against the developed countries, much as Algeria has already begun doing in the 1970s. The relationship that African states should have with the developed world as they grapple with their resource problems is a topic that will divide political forces within the continent. As during the early postcolonial days, splits on a major issue of external relations will provide an opportunity for domestic opposition groups to seek African allies and for continental leadership claimants to encourage the establishment of national governments that share their viewpoint. The crisis can also provide these leaders with followers if the latter's resentment can be turned against the developed world, or it could weaken the leader's appeal if the resentment of impoverished countries is turned against them. The choice among alternatives is not obvious. It is likely that it will depend a good deal on the success of the developing African states in maintaining their own socioeconomic growth and the success of developed countries in co-opting the more powerful states.

## GENERATIONAL SUCCESSION

The second important element in analyzing African trends concerns generational succession. When the 1980s begin, nearly all of Africa will still be ruled by one of two generational "classes": The Independence Generation, or the Class of 1918 (the mean birth year of the heads of state), and the Military Generation, or the Class of 1931. During the 1980s, two other generations will come into prominence: the Postindependence Generation, also part of the Class of 1931, which now rules in a very few states; and the Civic Generation, or the Class of 1945. In the interests of identification, the name and date of the leadership cohort are drawn from the head of state; obviously, almost all of his or her team in power is younger, often considerably younger. No one would expect them all to die or otherwise leave office when the leader does. Yet it is not inaccurate to speak of a cohort, since the leadership team shares attitudes, experiences, and identities; and changes in personnel and viewpoint at the top often involve important changes down the line.

A third of the 20 African states ruled in 1978 by the Independence Generation—who participated in struggles against colonial rule and were the first heads of government after the colonizers left—will be out of office when the 1980s begin, and many of the rest will disappear during the decade (those remaining coming mainly from the six states that have or will have attained independence in the 1970s). Replacement will occur generally in one of two ways. Normal succession by the Postindependence Generation (as has already occurred in Morocco, Gabon, and Liberia) will bring a younger member of the incumbent team, who has been trained on the job, into office through designation by the predecessor, acceptance by colleagues, and then approval by plebiscite. Although in some cases there will be a direct normal succession (as in the above-named cases), in others there will be an interim normal succession from among the Independence or Postindependence Generation, followed by the accession of a younger person of the Civic Generation (e.g., Minister Hedi Nouira followed by Party Director Mohammed Sayah in Tunisia). Since the leaders of the Independence Generation are venerable figures, it will be difficult for them to retire. They will age, eventually die in office, and be replaced by a considerably younger cohort. The later succession occurs, the greater the chances of jumping the Postindependence Generation and bringing in the Civic Generation directly (e.g., the succession of President Leopold Sedar Senghor, born in 1906, by Prime Minister Abdou Diouf, born in 1935, in Senegal).

The Military Generation, through military succession, will continue to replace the Independence Generation, although its mean birth year will gradually move up as time goes on. Some of the 20 military regimes in place in the 1970s can be expected to stay in the 1980s. They are Nasserite in temperament, opposed to pluralistic party competition but unable to set up a working single party, committed to programs of order and austerity achieved through an alliance of military and civilian technicians, and convinced of the need for government free of the burdens of popular accountability rather than of a return to procedural democracy. Yet military regimes will be increasingly going out of style in the 1980s as the incumbent military and governed populations alike learn that the military can, at best, clean up the mess of the Independence Generation but cannot govern any better than their predecessors; in fact, it will become apparent to both that the military is not particularly suited to meeting the very problems that need most attention: problems of movement, not problems of order. Since political choices are generally not made on the basis of all alternatives but rather in reaction to the most immediate past events, the more established the military regime and the longer the time since the latest military coup, the more likely will be preparations for civilian turnover. Military Generation leaders who have grown old in office are likely to be satisfied with having eliminated the Independence Generation but weary of the responsibility of governing; like other military establishments, they will retire to a guardian role. (In the lands of the more recent coups—whether single or repetitive—the military will still be in power, as explained above.)

In the mid-1970s the 30-year-old Civic Generation is nowhere to be found in power, but for all practical purposes it will be leading many governments in the 1980s, either as a result of civilian restoration or as a continuation of the process of normal succession (members of the Civic Generation are not likely to be heads of many states during the 1980s, but are likely to dominate government from the prime ministry on down). The Civic Generation is well educated, civilian, oriented toward order and efficiency, nationalist more in the sense of seeking self-reliance than of aspiring to equality with the former colonizer, and concerned with the substance more than with the symbols of development. (The term *Civic* is designed to reflect these traits, rather than suggest an idealized virtue.) Members of this generation will combine characteristics of the presently opposite types of politician and technician, although not always without strains.

As civilians, they will need a party behind them. As the nationalist-movement-turned-single-party was the dominant political institution of the Independence and the Postindependence generations, and the army council the characteristic organ of the Military Generation, so the competitive party system will be typical of the Civic Generation. The Civic Generation will need a new, supportive institution, more of an electoral than a mobilization organization, linked to parliamentary or executive factions seeking a public sounding board or legitimizer behind their policies. Since policy, personality, region, and possibly even social alliance in some cases will provide the basis for differences on issues, there are likely to be competing parties. There will be more people available for competing leadership groups because a larger population will receive secondary and higher education, often even beyond the absorptive capacity of the employment market. Competition is not always going to be on the basis of equality, to be sure; it will certainly involve temporary dominance by one party or another, charges of disloyal opposition, party splits and purges, and other vicissitudes of pluralistic politics.

Competitive parties will arise from either scission in the nationalist single party or the electoral efforts of parliamentary factions, the two classical sources of competitive party systems. Whatever their source, the parties are likely to be haunted by their antecedents and will be pressed to shake off the leftovers of the nationalist movement and its ethnic subdivisions (problems that overcame efforts in Ghana and Benin in the 1960s to replace the Military Generation with competitive parties, even if not with successive generations).

There is a difference between the attitudes of those born before 1930 to 1935 who grew up working together for independence and were still young enough upon its attainment to fill positions of power, and the attitudes of the next cohort, born before 1945–1950, who received their secondary education in the national school system and then climbed up the national ladders of employment as best they could, considering that the preceding cohort had a firm hold on the top positions. In political systems where expectations are generally satisfied, attitudes are formed in positive response and emulation of going practices, but where expectations are not met, attitudes favor antithetical practices and values. Civilians of the Postindependence Generation and their military counterparts tend to see leadership deficiency as a major domestic problem but, ironically, have little faith in democracy and the people's voice; they see foreign problems in an East-West context and look for only gradual regional integration within Africa. Members of the Civic Generation appear as technicians who see mass underdevelopment as a major political problem but who, also ironically, have faith in democracy and "the people" and reject authoritarian methods of government; foreign problems are seen in a North-South context, and regional unity is considered a priority political goal. Such changes in attitude show a reassuring vitality in the political process as people react to current failures of single-party and military regimes by seeking an answer to problems in "opposite" types of regimes and activities, although such positive attitudes, if unrequited, may turn into cynicism toward all political activity or later to even greater regimentation as the only way to restructure society.

Not only the ideology but also the geographical base of the ruling elites can be expected to change. Power bases will shift as previously ignored regions and ethnic groups are increasingly brought into the processes of development. Two contradictory trends are conceivable, and both are likely to occur. On the one hand, non-"peripheral" elements from outlying regions and subordinate ethnic groups may develop enough to challenge the established national leadership. (The predominance of the Akans in the Ivory Coast, the Kikuyu in Kenya, and the Sahilis in Tunisia is likely to go the way of the Amharas of Ethiopia, the Hausas of Nigeria, or the Coastals of Madagascar, although not necessarily by violent overthrow.) As new groups begin to benefit from development and become more fully integrated into the modernizing society, economy, and polity, they will begin to compete for political control as a means of acquiring larger shares of scarce resources.

On the other hand, indigenous populations in the burgeoning cities—as well as the migrants from rural areas who also occupy them—are likely to try to maintain government in the city, by the city, and for the city. Since education is the key to government service and entry to education is easiest for urban dwellers, government is likely to stay in urban hands and reflect urban interests. The rest of the country will benefit and indeed will participate in politics only as it comes to the city, and so urban migration will continue unabated. African cities are growing faster than the total population and will double their size at independence by the end of the 1980s, or earlier in some cases.

Exaggerated urban growth is a sign of rural neglect and also a sign that rural populations would rather switch than fight their neglect at the hands of government.

But a city is dependent on outside sources of supply, either from the countryside or from abroad. It is less resilient than the countryside, since it cannot simply go back to nature and feed itself, and it needs a more complex and diversified supply of goods and services. Thus the city must make some arrangement—exploitive or cooperative—with its hinterland, or it must increase its own dependency on the outside world. Since such dependency is not without cost, urban-monopolized political systems must find something to give their external donors. In Africa they generally have little. The only available goods are political support and raw materials—either tropical products or minerals—and since the latter are found in rural areas, not in the city, they, too, require control and exploitation of the countryside. Yet it will be evident to the urban governing elites that development is not measured by the size of the capital alone or by its architectural resemblance to metropolitan cities. As a result, decentralization is likely to become a common policy, not as a rural development measure but as an effort of secondary urbanization. It will be directed from the capital but will provide the basis for growing regional interests and pluralism.

In social and political terms, a government needs allies, groups who will benefit from its rule and support it. In many African countries in the mid-1970s, these allies are regional groups or tribes, geopolitical rather than sociopolitical entities. Rulers in Cameroon, Zaire, Sudan, Benin, the Ivory Coast, Madagascar, Senegal, Guinea, Algeria, Morocco, and elsewhere have established a durable political regime by a careful balance of regional and ethnic interests. The same type of policy is likely to be important in Africa in the 1980s, just as all regional and ethnic representation is important today in the United States. Detribalized politics is not likely to be a characteristic of most African states in this century. But governments also need allies among social groups that cut across ethnic or regional identifications.

In most cases, the peasantry will not be among these allies, although it will continue to make up the majority of the population in all African countries. An effective rural party or rural-party competition is just as unlikely to appear as a peasant revolutionary organization, since in most cases widespread agricultural—and, generally, rural—modernization, organization, and integration into the national market are not likely to have proceeded far enough to bring the peasantry actively into politics as an independent force. Except in North Africa, the continent is not ready for a Green Revolution in any sense of the term. Exceptions could also occur where a regime falls to tribal leaders whose member-followers are largely rural or where it falls to "Maoist" leaders with a pro-rural "bootstrapping" ideology for self-reliance (as in Tanzania or Guinea-Bissau).

But in many countries, particularly the developing societies of Africa, enough development will have taken place to give rise to some incipient functional interest groups that will provide an urban coalition as a governmental alliance. Such groups will vary greatly according to the makeup of the particular country, but business, labor, and civil service sectors are likely to develop both general corporate identities and an awareness of their own particular interests. There are few countries, however, in which these groups will be strong enough to be independent allies of government rather than vulnerable, controllable sources of support.

It would be hard to be more precise and carry an identification of future elite divisions and interests much further. Nevertheless, it is clear that the inherent immobility of the great coalition of the single party's Great Coalition and of the military regime's order- and consumption-oriented army and bureaucracy is likely to be replaced, wherever it exists, by a more coherent modernizing urban coalition with complementary interests that will favor economic growth and productive distribution.

## SUBREGIONAL LEADERSHIP AND GROUPS

A vital element in determining the economic and political behavior of African states—particularly in relation to the North— is its own regional, i.e., continental, pattern of relations. The regional system of the period since 1963, in which matters of common interest and disputes among the system members are handled by regular meetings and ad hoc mediation, has been of the concern type. There is a broad consensus on norms and identities; firm alliances and a reaction of counteralliances are excluded. This arrangement is essentially a collective-security system and is quite successful in dealing with the "middle level" of inter-African relations: conflict and even some cooperation among the African states. Serious problems of boundaries, alleged interventions, and other cases of "bad blood" among African states have been mediated within the framework of—although not actually by—the Organization of African Unity (OAU), the institutionalized form of the regional system, to the point where it can be said that the system can manage interstate conflict whenever it reaches a certain threshold of intensity.

That threshold may be as high as a brief war of exhaustion from which the parties cannot extricate themselves without systematic mediation (as in the Moroccan-Algerian and Somalian-Ethiopian wars of 1963–1964), but it is more likely to lie far short of war and even of informal hostilities. The only exceptions since 1964 have been the Tanzanian-supported attack on Uganda in 1973, when forces favorable to exiled Ugandan President Milton Obote, who had been ousted in a coup by Idi Amin, mounted an unsuccessful countercoup from Tanzanian soil; the Algerian-based attack in 1976–1978 on the former Spanish Sahara which had been partitioned between Morocco and Mauritania; and the 1977–1978 conquest of eastern Ethiopia by Somalia. When the states of the region reach the more advanced stages of the struggle for predominance analyzed earlier, this conflict-managing capability may erode, although even then it may still operate when conflicts are among followers of the same leadership.

African conflict management frequently operates through the mediation of other African states outside the conflict subregion. Its operation does not depend on this characteristic, however, and future conflict management could effectively evolve in a number of directions: through the use of mediators from other subregions, to strengthen continental interaction; through mediators from within the conflict subregion, to strengthen subregional cohesion; or through mediators from within non-subregional leadership blocs, to strengthen their cohesion. There are precedents for all these patterns in the first 15 years of independence.

The regional system is plagued, however, by an inability to decide on other appropriate tasks and by a lack of power necessary to handle these tasks if it does identify them. It has been unsuccessful, often frustratingly so, in coordinating effective policy among African states toward the exterior world, including their paramount external goal of eliminating the southern racist redoubt. This failure at the "upper" level of relations was a constant annoyance to the system members during the decade between Rhodesia's Unilateral Declaration of Independence from Great Britain in 1965 and the military coup in Portugal of 1974. The subsequent independence of Angola and Mozambique—in which outside African states had little role, since it was won by indigenous nationalist movements and granted by Portugal's new leadership—and the consequent encirclement of Rhodesia with sovereign black states by 1976 have provided the system with a new opportunity for extraregional involvement in African problems as well as a new regional arena of inter-African relations.

The second type of problem that has frustrated the continental system is at the lower level of relations: conflicts within one African state that have serious inter-African ramifications. Despite their declared norm of nonintervention in such internal affairs, the African states are continuously drawn in by their values of African solidarity and by the nature of the OAU as a "heads of states' club." Unable to respond effectively either to opportunities for peacemaking or to appeals for support by the beleaguered head of state, the OAU members are paralyzed and the activities of the Organization blocked until the crisis is over. Their inability to solve problems they should not be solving weakens their ability to solve other problems (such as those at the upper level), as was shown during the period from 1965 (the time of the second Congo crisis) to 1970 (the end of the Biafran war) and again in 1976, when the OAU split over Angola.

Such strains at the upper and lower levels of inter-African relations are also closely related to the future potential for leadership rivalries, since they provide issues for competition over strategies.

The three levels of conflict solving are also related to the subregional pattern of relations in Africa. Underneath a structure of growing relations on the continental level is a developing network of subregional relations. Since the 1960s, linguistic groupings and barriers have tended to break down, geographic (subregional) groupings have gradually risen in importance, and ideological groups have disappeared but may well try to re-emerge. The first trend is natural and certain to continue; linguistic groups and barriers are a colonial heritage and prevent neighbors with common features and problems from cooperating or from overcoming conflicts. Where subregional cooperation can be a continuation or extension of preindependence patterns (ex-British East Africa, ex-French Equatorial Africa, ex-French North Africa), such continuity is all to the good, for it strengthens current efforts, but in most of the continent buttressing regional groupings requires overcoming colonial separations.

The second trend—the rise of subregional cooperation—has been a characteristic of the OAU period. Since the founding of the OAU in 1963, African states' contacts within their subregion or with their neighbors have generally been twice as frequent as diplomatic contacts on the continental level. Most of the diplomatically active African states have concentrated the majority of their contacts within their subregion, and subregional business tends to be handled by visits from government officials (often at cabinet level) rather than by regular diplomatic missions.

The third trend is the limited appearance of ideological groups. The OAU was formed to reconcile the ideological splits that prevented African states from taking common action. To the extent that continental leadership struggles are translated into a search for alliances that break up the concert system, ideological groupings can be expected to return. Yet unlike the inchoate bipolar pattern of the early 1960s (the moderate Brazzaville group versus the more radical Casablanca group), which gave way to the OAU concert, the ideological alliances of the 1980s will have to come to terms with the deeper underlying reality of closer subregional cooperation that has been growing to date.

Ideological ties may well strain and even disrupt the cooperation, but they will also be attentuated by it. To be sure, one may cite the examples of former French West Africa or former British East Africa, where a real interdependence existing among neighbors under colonial rule was discarded, without consideration of cost, under the influence of ideology and sovereign independence—a policy that will be just as possible in the 1980s. But however possible, it may be less likely, if only because the new subregionalism is the result of freely adopted national policy rather than a structure imposed from abroad.

Nevertheless, within these limitations, the development of subregionalism is likely to form one of the predominant patterns of inter-African relations in the 1980s. Subregionalism means working together with neighbors on common development efforts and common problems, but it also means, by that very fact, pulling away from the efforts and problems of other subregions and hence of the continent as a whole. Although in some corners of Africa subregionalism means a gradual organization of subregional institutions and an agreement on their appropriate tasks, in the south the problems of subregional function and organization are more basic and more complex. Here colonial conditioning is still fresh, ideological differences are especially great, violence is an approved form of power, there is no precedent for subregional organization, and the liberation struggle is likely to bring out strong disagreements over tactics and leadership.

Liberation may be a precondition for development, but the two have generally proven to be antithetical issues, not necessarily incompatible in their demands but competing in their focus. Thus the nature and interests of the southern African subregion are significantly different from those of the rest of the continent. By 1980 Rhodesia will doubtless be Zimbabwe, with a moderate or a radical government depending on whether the means of liberation are primarily diplomatic or military. Namibia, too, is likely to be independent, an underdeveloped territory serving as both a bridge and a buffer between Angola and South Africa, but almost necessarily in conflict with one or the other.

The main focus of attention will be on South Africa in the decade of the 1980s. Debate will rage among the three points of view: that of the African revolutionaries and their African and external allies, who seek to destroy white South Africa; that of the South African liberals and their external allies and African sympathizers, who would like to negotiate a transition to a multiracial society but are unable to find an *inter locuteur valable* of sufficient weight, no matter how imaginative they may be in devising structural solution; and that of the South African hardliners, with possibly a few external sympathizers, who find reason for their stand in the strength of the revolutionaries and the weakness of the liberals. The revolution already began, in Soweto in June 1976, when South African youths spontaneously showed that they had no material inhibitions or fears restraining their recourse to violence. In addition to the revolution and external pressure, the South African problem will also involve the black tribal homelands (Bantustans), many of which will have become restive "little Lesothos" by 1980; the homelands will be more and more torn between their dependence on South Africa, within which they lie as fragmented enclaves, and their supposed independence. Their populations will increasingly taunt their leaders with such a contradiction.

Thus, the liberation issue will turn into a hot dispute over diplomatic versus military means, providing a major policy difference for continental leadership rivalries to exploit. At the same time, to a greater extent than ever, the liberation issue even in its final phase is likely to be less appealing to other subregions than it is to the South, particularly as the subregions gradually coalesce around their own developmental issues. This can already be seen in the Zimbabwe confrontation, in which the five neighboring subregional states—the front-line countries of Angola, Mozambique, Zambia, Tanzania, and Botswana—have taken a more active role than stronger states elsewhere on the continent.

Although it is easier to predict the dynamics of continental interaction than to sharpen the focus on the future of the subregions, some of their characteristics stand out. North, West, and Central Africa each have their giant, around which cooperation will center or against which it will be directed. Algeria, Nigeria, and Zaire, respectively, are necessarily the dominant partners in their regions, even if they are as timid as Nigeria has been in times past. In addition to their economic and demographic weight, their central geographic position in the subregion shapes their role. Institutionalized cooperation in North Africa will be on Algeria's terms or it will not exist; in West Africa, it can exist without, and to some degree against, Nigeria; and any groups formed in Central Africa without Zaire will be sufficiently weak for some member always to be tempted to seek a strengthening alliance with the giant.

To expand on these predictions by region: North Africa in the 1980s is likely to be as ridden with divisive rivalries among its three or four states as it has been in the past (whether Algeria succeeds in dethroning the Sherifian monarchy or not), in a Kautilyan pattern of relations in which neighbors are enemies and neighbors' neighbors are allies. North African countries all have a good chance of continued development and are likely to expand their contacts with Europe as they seek greater acceptance by and equality with the developed world. This policy will either pull them away from the rest of Africa or lead them to use other African states as troops in their campaign.

In West Africa, the Ivory Coast is likely to lead a group of medium and small states in restrained competition with another group of very small states led by Nigeria (for aid, markets, investment capital, and international maneuverability), each group containing both French- and English-speaking members—whether this competition takes place within a general West African economic community or between two such organizations. Although important political questions in the area concern the maintenance of civilian regimes in the key French-speaking states of Senegal and the Ivory Coast and the return to civilian rule in the key English-speaking states of Ghana and Nigeria, these questions are not likely to have a major effect on the patterns of subregional relations. Only three or possibly four states—Nigeria, the Ivory Coast, Liberia, and possibly Ghana—have real chances of development, and in the process they will produce a wide gap between the growing modern sector and the rest of the population even if efforts are made to attenuate that distinction. The other countries will produce more equalitarian societies, with lower expectations and lower realizations, but they will also continue to export large segments of their populations to the developing states, a movement that can increase subregional cooperation and also tension. In other words, increased subregionalism in West Africa will be based on a real increase in interests and interactions but will involve times of tension as well as increases in cooperation, probably troubled less by differences in ideologies and regimes than by substantive conflicts.

In Central Africa, the pivotal states are likely to be Zaire and, secondarily, Cameroon, but relationships there are not likely to be as highly institutionalized as in West Africa. Indeed, ideological differences, as between a revolutionary Congo and a neocolonialist Gabon, and differences in development strategy, as between a poor desert Chad and the more balanced growth of Cameroon, are likely to keep the sense of subregionalism more subdued in this area than elsewhere.

In East Africa, polar states are lacking and so a Kautilyan pattern is most likely to occur. As in the Maghreb but at a much lower level of development, the core states of East Africa are near equals, and they will probably continue as rivals even after the passing of Idi Amin from Uganda. The ideological differences of free enterprise Kenya and rural socialist Tanzania, both showing some substantial growth, are likely to continue through any changes of regime, providing continued tensions to plague institutionalized cooperation. On some of its flanks (north and west), the East African subregion is hemmed in by geography and neighboring conflict zones, and so its members are condemned to interact together, even if cooperation is mixed with conflict. But to the south, new subregional boundaries may be drawn, as Tanzania complements its political and ideological attraction to Mozambique or even to Zambia and Zimbabwe with economic cooperation in markets, services, infrastructures, and supports. In the Horn of Africa, the field of conflict and alliance is likely to extend north and east to Sudan, Egypt, and Arabia rather than into black Africa.

In all these subregions, various types of disagreements are likely to hamper increasing cooperation from time to time, providing subregional or other states with the occasion to mediate and restore harmony. None of these characteristics is likely to be changed by any state fusions that may occur. Such mergers are hardest of all to predict. The very outlandishness of a Gambia, an Equatorial Guinea, a Djibouti, or a Cabinda (an Angolan enclave between Congo and Zaire) gives support to their existence; they are small territories, easy for their own leaders to control, and armor-plated with sovereignty. Natural economic clusters, with central circulation systems and goods to evacuate or exchange—such as Senegal, Mauritania, and Mali; or Ivory Coast and Upper Volta; or Nigeria, Benin, and Niger; or Kenya and Uganda; or Malawi, Mozambique, and Zimbabwe—may or may not turn their economic complementarity into political cooperation, but such moves will depend on political perceptions and goals, not on economics. No such moves hovered on the horizon of the mid-1970s; for them to occur in the 1980s, changes in incumbent governments will almost certainly be required. Similarly, it will take more than a decade and a half for any of the loose subregional cooperation institutions to come to grips with their serious differences and decide to overcome them by conscious integration policies, if indeed that is to be their response. These institutions include the 4- or 5-state Central African Economic and Customs Union (UDEAC), founded in 1966; the 3-member East African Community (EAC), which functioned from 1963 to 1977; the 15-state Economic Community of West African states founded in 1975 and, within it, the 4- or 5-member Council of the Entente, founded in 1959, and the 6-member Economic Community of West Africa (CEAO), founded in 1972, to name the more durable or more structured among them.

As subregional interaction proceeds, continental interaction—and its organizational forum, the OAU—is expected to diminish in relative importance and, if anything, fall prey to the previously analyzed continental leadership struggle. The interplay between these two levels is likely to have some real implications for the stance of individual African states in the North-South dialogues. Although it has been suggested that a realistic awareness of problems and a pragmatic approach to solutions are likely to characterize both the new Civic Generation and the growing subregional configurations, such attitudes may well be contested

99

during regional struggles for continental dominance and Third World influence. Radical leadership, intervention in internal African affairs, support for liberation movements in southern Africa, and a tough North-South stance are likely to gravitate upward to the continental level, while moderate leadership, interstate cooperation, stress on development, and more flexible diplomatic positions generally are likely to be found on the subregional levels—except, of course, in southern Africa. Elsewhere subregional groupings are unlikely to be ideological, since the conditions and viewpoints of member states will differ considerably. Undeniably, this element will add strains and disunity to African states' stands in North-South negotiations, disunity that in turn will fuel attempts at ideological leadership as a unifying force.

## EXTERNAL PENETRATION

Foreign relations of the African territories in colonial times were structured around interaction with the metropole—more strictly so in the case of the Spanish-, Portuguese-, and French-speaking territories than in the case of the British. In the 1960s and 1970s, the major trend has been the attenuation of this bilateral pattern. On occasion a new bilateralism has appeared when the former metropole has been replaced by one of the cold war protagonists, but in most cases colonial bilateralism has given way to multilateralism and a diversification of relations.

*Multilateralism* refers here to relations between groups of countries, more specifically to arrangements in which the direct link from non-African to African and other Third World states is mediated by the need for prior collective agreement within each of the two groupings. The relations between the European Economic Community and the African adherents of the Yaoundé and Lomé Conventions are a good example, as are relations between developed-country consumers and Third World commodity-producers' groups (such as OPEC and the copper group) or between the developed-country minority and the Third World majority in the UN. The balance within each group lies between collective interest and individual direction; each member must weigh the chances of increased support for its own interests against the danger of dilution by the preponderance of others' interests (a consideration illustrated dramatically by the OPEC price split at the end of 1976). Multilateralism enhances national power by pooling choices and interests.

*Diversified relations* refers here to relations between a single African state and a number of other non-African states on a particular matter. As a successor to bilateralism, diversification replaces one source of relations with several, dependency with alternatives, and the promise of fidelity with the threat of going elsewhere as the major source of power; it enhances national autonomy by extending the freedom to maneuver. The shopping around for arms that frequently characterizes African military purchases—as in Morocco, Somalia, Tanzania, or Nigeria—is an example that is likely to continue wherever possible.

If bilateralism characterized the colonial relationship, a changing mixture of all three types of interaction is now typical of the relations of African states and in fact of independent states in general. Thus, in the 1980s, some African countries may well still be in the franc zone, but it also likely that the franc will be in the Monnet zone (that of the new European currency, named after a European Community founding father), a few African countries will be in African monetary zones (e.g., Benin and Niger joining Nigeria), and the rest—like all other former members of colonial monetary zones—will be on their own.

In general, bilateralism will continue for a long time in certain language-related cultural matters of secondary (but not zero) political importance. For many Africans of states in their second independent decade, the choice of foreign university, foreign military academy, foreign business network, perhaps even foreign aid program will be oriented by considerations of language and prestige toward the former metropole. Such exclusivity will be challenged wherever Africans have something—students, soldiers, business, even development—that is of interest to others, and diversification will ensue. Common language will also become an instrument of diversification as Africans make use of it to expand ties with foreign states that were not their colonizers, as an entrée into great-power politics or a means of alliance with foreign states that already have ties elsewhere within their subregion. Thus Nigerians will go to college in America, Angolans will receive aid from Cuba, and citizens of Niger will attend the Ivory Coast military academy.

Although both colonial return and the establishment of exclusive ties between sovereign states are conceivable, such new instances of bilateralism are unlikely to take place. Both power considerations—the inability of an outside country to take and hold a colony now—and the norms of international politics militate against a new colonialism. As for new satellite relations, neither the assumed continuity of détente nor the norms of nationalist sovereignty permit a superpower to establish an African client regime. Even the governments of Zaire and Angola in the mid-1970s, for all their closeness to the United States and the U.S.S.R., respectively, were not satellites of the superpowers.

By the same token it is also likely that African diversification of relations in the 1980s will not simply be cold war bilateralism in disguise, in which the diversified partners are merely the Northern allies of one dominant superpower. Instead, the present trend of increasing exchanges with all Northern states will continue. Even states such as the Ivory Coast or Angola, which shunned the Soviet Union and the United States, respectively, until the mid-1970s, will have opened up to everybody a decade later. This does not mean, of course, that momentary clashes and huffs will be a thing of the past, or that all African states will have exactly the same types of relations with all Northern states. Particularly as the continental struggle for leadership evolves, and as domestic factions scuffle over scarce resources, governments will look for external support and may be temporarily identified with one leading Northern state or another. But as in the case of Algeria, Tanzania, or Senegal in the 1970s, the Africans are likely to try to diversify their relations with the North and vice versa in order to gain maximum benefits and leverage.

If the general trend from bilateralism toward diversification is the characteristic structural pattern, what about multilateralization? There are numerous opportunities for African states to band together to face the North: commodity groups, subregional groups, the regional group of the OAU, ideological alliances, postcolonial client groups (such as independent members of the British Commonwealth), and membership in the Group of 77 (the"club" of most of the states of the South). Yet, in fact, there are grounds to doubt the effectiveness of any but the subregional groups in dealing with the North.

The Southern bloc of the 77 is effective in starting confrontations and keeping negotiations going; but once these negotiations get to specifics, the interests within the two "sides" vary so much according to particular topics that the Southern members have a hard time hanging together. The problem with new commodity groups following on the heels of OPEC is rather the opposite. Their common interests are generally too narrow, so that participating states are not cohesive enough in other respects; and the commodities involved do not have the clout that oil does. Coffee, cocoa, copper, manganese, and possibly even uranium agreements are likely to be negotiated with African producers' participation, to be sure, and perhaps even with revenue-stabilization provisions in some cases, but without the drastic price hikes or effective market-control mechanisms of oil diplomacy.

Within the continent alone, the OAU can be expected to concentrate its already strained capacities on regional problem solving, while being torn by the coming continental leadership struggle, as discussed earlier. Postcolonial groupings will continue to lose importance. The Commonwealth will maintain restricted contacts, and the French-speaking club may meet from time to time with small effect.

From the European point of view, the evolution of African-European relations can be expected to continue its trend toward generalized preferences without special treatment for Africa; the second and last Lomé Agreement, to be signed in 1981, will merely be a commercial agreement with some aid provisions and a larger stabilization account than the first one had, but without any more specific European provisions for preferential trade for

Africa. By its expiration in the mid-1980s, the North will have generalized some of these provisions to the entire South and let the rest drop.

The multilateral organization most likely to deal effectively with the North is the subregional association, which combines political commitment and complementary interests to provide a relatively cohesive collectivity. As discussed earlier, subregional groupings vary according to the area in question, but their potential is great in every corner of the continent. Within subregional groups, states can coordinate or legislate the forms, conditions, and limits of foreign penetration and can increase the effectiveness of their decisions by action in concert. In regard to external penetration as well as to relations among themselves, subregional clusters present a positive-sum situation. The member states have little to lose and much to gain, whether they are weaker or stronger, underdeveloping or developing.

The final question on the structure of relations concerns the conditions of change. In what matters will the move from bilateralism be accomplished through the maintenance of good relations and hence the chance of further benefits from the bilateral partner, and in what matters will it involve confrontation and rupture of relations, posing a sudden challenge to domestic capabilities? There are very few instances of notably tightened relations between African states and their former metropole (e.g., Mali in 1968). Instead, states move toward diversified relations either through gradual erosion or as a result of a sudden change in government or an incident. Natural erosion has already been taking place; it will continue, and changes in attitude will follow. Political elites are less likely to be Euro-centered or Northwardly oriented; indeed, Africa may well undergo a heavy wave of xenophobia. Expatriate advisers and business leaders may be considered as much of an anomaly as was colonial rule in the preceding generation; many types of foreign consumer goods will be disdained in favor of national products and styles; Africanization, nationalization, and decolonization will be major policy concerns.

But to the extent that there is natural erosion, the chances of hostile ruptures and confrontation decrease, since there is no longer the single target of the metropole on which to focus. Of course, the issues of poverty and redistribution still remain, and they are the basic matters of discussion in the North-South dialogue. But once the problem-solving phase of that dialogue has arrived, they are no longer ideological issues and can be broken down into technical details susceptible to being treated one at a time.

In addition to categorizing the structure of relations between African and non-African (Northern) countries, it is relevant to assess the degree of relations—or really of penetration, since power imbalance among the parties is certain to continue. At one pole is isolation; at the other, integration. Neither pole seems realistic; instead, a mixture of intermediate relations is to be expected. For example, Africa and the North will continue to exchange raw materials for industrial goods or money for arms at exchange rates that will vary according to political and economic components of the market. Africa will continue to receive capital transfers through aid and investment, sharing of technology, and other means—which they will generally deem insufficient. By the 1980s, a Western debt moratorium is possible, permitting new indebtedness all over again, but perhaps more likely is a more selective relationship in which the more attractive countries will either suspend debt payments or fall under creditor control over their economic operations. Northerners will continue to reside in African countries but in reduced numbers and under increased, although often insufficient, controls.

In the area of personnel particularly, a number of changes can be expected in the 1980s. Foreign troops are likely to be removed from Africa by the 1980s, although there may always be occasions for intervention and temporary stationing (see the scenarios at the end of the paper). There are not likely to be any mutual-defense agreements, although there may be some "friendship treaties" and there will be many training and military assistance agreements with the former metropole or with China, Russia, or the United States. Foreign civilian populations will be reduced to less than 0.5 percent of the total population, and in states that opt for a more self-reliant policy few foreigners will be welcome at all, even as technical advisers. Even tourism is likely to flourish in only a few states because tourism requires special natural resources, heavy specific investments, and a particular policy commitment. As a result, most African states are simply going to have fewer direct contacts with foreigners on their own soil than in the recent past (a fact that incidentally may reinforce subregional relations, since Africans are likely to see more of their neighbors than of the outside world). However, contrary to previous local experience, Africans who become managers in foreign corporations will make their contacts with the outside world through training visits and inspection trips.

Smaller foreign populations in Africa do not necessarily mean a small foreign commercial presence. Africanization of capital ownership is likely to increase, either through outright nationalization or through majority participation in joint enterprises. Yet, despite these measures, investment and commercial representation may very well continue to increase, even if less rapidly than needed for economic takeoff in most cases. Africanized or not, investment levels will vary greatly according to the host's market, resource possibilities, and policy climate. Some states because of small markets, scarce resources, or hostile policies, will be far down the scale toward isolation, while others will have active contacts with the world economic system, under varying degrees of national control.

In the field of education, there will be few non-Africans in the national universities as teachers or students, although there will still be many Africans in European, American, and even Asian universities as students and some as teachers. The linguistic debate will be hot and heavy, and unresolved. A third of the African states will have adopted an African language as their official language and will be in various states of linguistic transformation, while others will be resolutely pursuing the conversion of national communication into English, French, or Portuguese.

As a result, a few African activities will be reevaluated—i.e., be able to command a higher economic return or be of greater political weight in relation to the activities of other states—although dramatic changes do not seem likely. Industrialization will have produced some transformed raw materials or light industrial exports for higher prices; commodity agreements or producers' fiat will have produced higher rates for a few products; political competition among African states and among outside suppliers seeking influence will create some conditions for slightly improved terms on arms; and whatever evolution international organizations such as the UN may have undergone will produce somewhat greater need for African votes to pass international legislation. But these are not major changes in the international terms of trade, and judged by what the Africans feel they need, want, or are entitled to have, the values for their goods and services will continue to be insufficient. At the same time, African controls over foreign operators will have increased as host states become more aware and surer of their powers of sovereignty. Consequently, since African states will not be able to attract additional foreign activity but will be able to control it more stringently, the net result is often likely to be a reduction of foreign penetration and a need for increased self-reliance.

This characteristic fits in with others already noted: the rise of the Civic Generation, the development of subregional attempts at coordinated problem solving, and even a consequent attempt to use ideology as a broader umbrella under which to group adherents of continental leaders. But generally, although some annoying vestiges of "authentistic" symbolism (the substitution of "Africanisms," even if they need to be invented, for things deemed Western) will remain, leading African states are likely to be fed up with their own symbolism and to make genuine efforts to solve basic problems. Until the mid-1970s, African states tended to bring their problems to the North and impose enough pressure for a solution to be forthcoming which they could then ratify. The trend in which African states propose their own answers to their own problems—or their own terms for Northern help—is already beginning and likely to develop in full in the 1980s. Whether this trend will mean the formulation of technical programs for Northern help in meeting specific development problems or the reduction of internal demands and increase of supplies through local self-reliance without external help, it means that African states will continue to absorb more of technological civilization and fit its content to national forms. Those developing states that engage increasingly in diplomatic interaction with the Northern core will do so on their own terms and not as branch offices of the North. The other states will remain ghettos of benign neglect on the part of the outside world. In the 1980s total isolation is inconceivable, but in the past decade Africa has nonetheless experienced a greater degree of isolation than many other Third World areas and is likely to continue to do so.

In their participation in outside affairs, African states will join the rest of the world in the search for a new system of world order to replace the colonial and cold war system of the past. No model is available; and past patterns, such as balance of power, or future hopes, such as a world parliament, seem equally inapplicable. In the last quarter of the century, the world stands in an intermediate position, in which the sovereign equality of rights and the compensating inequality of needs of individuals and nations everywhere are being emphasized as never before, while effective equality of power to realize these universal demands is absent as usual. Despite its desires for planned order, the world of the 1980s is unlikely to do more than make some tentative preparations for the new millenium another decade away.

# TWO

# Scenarios

Over the preceding 15 years, the affairs of Africa were dominated by events that were foreseeable but not absolutely predictable. Although it makes unique sense in hindsight, the collapse of the Congo when the Belgians left in 1960 was neither sure nor incomprehensible nor possible only in the Congo; the same can be said of the discovery of oil on the continent, especially in Nigeria, and of the Biafran war. It does not make much sense to predict specific events for each of Africa's 47 countries. Any of them could, for example, break into pieces, stage a border claim or fall victim to one, invite the Russian Navy or Air Force (depending on the state's location) to set up bases, merge with its neighbor, or buy an atomic bomb and blackmail the rest of the world. To try to guess when and where is fruitless.

Instead it is more profitable to present two scenarios, which will be termed "eventful" and "uneventful." Both are related to the fortunes of détente, although it is impossible to say which is the independent variable, the status of détente at a given time or any of the events projected for Africa. The scenarios are also related to events in South Africa and, more specifically, most likely depend to a large extent on the way in which Zimbabwe obtains its independence.

## UNEVENTFUL SCENARIO

Zimbabwe achieves its independence before the end of the 1970s through a complicated diplomatic arrangement that gives Africans majority rule but leaves the whites with an assured position in national life. The agreement, negotiated at Lusaka with internal nationalist leaders, comes about through the combined pressure of the Carter regime, Britain, and Zambia, after increased guerrilla warfare has taken some toll of both sides and then ground to a stalemate of attrition. By the early 1980s, much of the white population has moved to South Africa, Brazil, and Australia; and the government has staged a coup, abrogated the previously negotiated constitution, and called for a constituent assembly that will write a new, one-man-one-vote constitution without special provisions to protect the whites.

A mixed group of young and old nationalists, drawn from the internal nationalists' alliance with parts of the national liberation army, comes to power under tension and skepticism from the outside. When the constitutional coup takes place, the older nationalists are eased out, and the Postindependence Generation, moderated by responsibility, comes to power. The country's economy is weaker than it was before independence, but production and consumption are in Zimbabwean hands and it recovers gradually at the end of the decade. Zimbabwe joins Zambia in developing political and economic cooperation, and the two eventually strengthen their exchanges with Malawi, Mozambique, and Tanzania. When elections take place in Malawi (after Banda's death) and Zimbabwe, the five-nation group takes the unusual step of supporting moderate socialist successors against some strong South African–oriented opposition from the original nationalists' groups, thus assuring a similarity of self-reliance policies in all five countries. Angola is busy showing that socialism in one country can work, although it takes a number of years before its authority is felt throughout the entire land. In other words, according to the first scenario, the radical belt of southern Africa turns its energies inward, toward basic problems of development.

The most striking series of events during the 1980s occurs in

South Africa. Considerable pressure is being maintained on South Africa since the United States was enlisted in the campaign, trading an understanding on investment against an understanding on social change. Also, the leaders of the Lebowa and Bophutatswana homelands have called for "formal partnership" in the country, and the government, despite its continued ability to contain urban youth unrest, is worried enough about the future to have proposed a number of serious institutional reforms leading to a federal state. Transkei and Kwazulu, once independent as homelands, have formed a Xhosa confederation with the states of Swaziland and Lesotho, although it has taken near intervention from the UN Security Council to protect the new state from South African interference; the confederation received large amounts of Northern aid.

Namibia has received its independence—on terms closer to those of South Africa than those of the UN-recognized nationalist representative, the South-West African People's Party (SWAPO)—but even though SWAPO has not been granted the majority black rule it desires, the new government incorporates many SWAPO elements. This government has improved ties not only with Angola but also with Botswana, which has a liberal economy. Both Namibia and the Xhosa Confederation have been recognized by African states and have become members of the OAU and the UN.

With all its ups and downs Soviet-American détente has continued to work during the 1980s. Although Russia announced support for revolution in southern Africa and promised to follow up with resources, there was little revolution to support, and eventually the Xhosa confederation crisis and the Zimbabwe and Namibian settlements showed that there was more to be gained by taking joint measures with America than by going alone. At the beginning of the 1980s, under pressure from the OAU through a resolution sponsored by Egypt, the Ivory Coast, Zaire, Tanzania, Senegal, and Morocco, the U.S.S.R. and Cuba withdrew all their troops from the continent and Russia then came to an understanding with the United States that neither country would have any troops or military technicians in Africa. Despite the Djibouti war, sketched out below, the agreement has held.

Outside of the guerrilla actions in Zimbabwe and Namibia, the continent has undergone a number of wars, although none has been as serious as the Djibouti war. The Ugandan invasion of Kenya after the death of President Kenyatta (during which much of the Ugandan Army defected and President Idi Amin was defeated and overthrown), the Tibesti war between Libya and Chad, and the three-sided war over Equatorial Guinea, among others, followed the normal course of past African wars: incidents, build-up, brief war, exhaustion, stalemate, mediation, return to status quo. The Djibouti war, however, became a testing ground for two major recipients of American and Soviet arms with perceived vital interests involved and with the incomplete episode of the Ogaden war of 1977–1978 (in which Somalis occupied part of Ethiopia) to terminate. The war broke out between Ethiopia and Somalia in the early 1980s, after five years of Djiboutian independence from France, and was triggered by a pro-Somali coup in the ministate. Hostilities continued until all the arms were exhausted and covert supplies of parts and replacements proved insufficient; at that point, the United States and the U.S.S.R. reaffirmed their previous agreement and extended it to cover direct intervention in an ongoing war. Under those conditions, the war quickly fell back to stalemate. An OAU commission proposed a territorial reallocation in the Horn of Africa which resulted in the definitive cession of the Ogaden area (formerly in Ethiopia) to Somalia, most of Djibouti territory to Ethiopia, and a free port with guaranteed transit for both countries in Djibouti itself, accompanied by a formal statement from Somalia that its irredentist claims had been satisfied. Soon afterward, King Hassan II of Morocco made a free-access arrangement with Algeria in regard to the phosphate port he was building at the mouth of the Dra River. After suitable deliberations, Algeria accepted. This left the territorial disputes in the Western Sahara completely settled, since Morocco had reduced the Polisario threat to its Saharan provinces to manageable proportions and then had ratified its 1972 border agreement with Algeria, which had cut its support to a losing cause.

Meanwhile, a number of economic communities have slowly and carefully taken shape on the continent. Although the Economic Community of West African States (ECOWAS) has continued to evolve slowly under the weight of Nigeria—which also developed a number of unequal economic cooperation arrangements with its neighbors Niger, Benin, and Togo—the West African Economic Community (CEAO) has changed shape somewhat in the process and developed more closely institutionalized economic cooperation among the nine states of the Western Quadrant: Senegal, the Ivory Coast, Mali, Upper Volta, Gambia, Guinea (after a military coup removed President Sékou Touré), Guinea-Bissau, Liberia, and Sierra Leone. The group has coordinated its planning, consulted before taking positions, abolished internal customs and therefore eliminated smuggling, set up a common external tariff, and began to employ joint UN representatives at economic debates. In Equatorial Africa, the Central African Economic and Customs Union (UDEAC) has continued to function and pull together, as Gabon, Congo, and Cameroon continued to develop and to narrow their ideological differences. In East Africa, after the abortive Ugandan invasion, Kenya and Uganda pursued cool relations, and Kenya has since become a prime and individual example of successful if chaotic economic liberalism. Although there is greater need in the south to consolidate national systems before embarking on mergers, the states of the Zambezi (Mozambique, Malawi, Zimbabwe, and Zambia) have set up a common authority to manage cooperation in the fields of labor, energy, and transport. Tanzania, finding no sympathetic partners in East Africa, has joined them.

The OAU itself, which has favored the formation of economic communities, has become less active in political disputes, except for its continuing role as a locus for mediation, but in early 1980s it launched a three-year cycle of conferences and studies designed to coordinate and disseminate improved educational programs. As economic cooperation within subregions has grown, linguistic groupings have become less practical. Most of the successful functioning organisms of the French-speaking African and Mauritian Common Organization (OCAM) have been transferred to the OAU.

The political systems of the continent vary mainly in relation to individual countries' economic fortunes. The smaller, poorer states remain under military rule or personal civilian dictatorship. In other states, such as Tanzania, Mozambique, the Ivory Coast, Kenya, Zaire, Liberia, Zambia, Guinea-Bissau, Cameroon, and Algeria, the single party continues to function. In the approximately half-dozen most rapidly developing states, societal cohesion, including a stable political regime, has been achieved by the absorbing of pluralistic competition for a growing pool of resources. The single party is at times a real channel of citizen participation and a force for unity, at other times merely a downward channel of control and propaganda. In all cases there is power in the party; people and ideas rise through its hierarchy, for the government then to coordinate and administer, and neither people nor ideas enter the political system except through the party. The party serves as an important framework for order and continuity when the founding father has passed on—as he has in all these states except Mozambique and Guinea-Bissau—and so is mythologized as the major source of legitimacy. In Ghana, Nigeria, Senegal, Tunisia, and Morocco, a working multiparty system formed the structure of politics. In Senegal and Tunisia, the new opposition party came to power in an election on the death of the founding father, and in Ghana and Nigeria, the military regimes had given way to civilian rule based on the new parties.

African states in general are using the prospects of mutually beneficial relations with the North to negotiate more favorable conditions for redistribution of wealth; multilateral negotiations concern technical conditions as well as general principles. By 1990 Algeria and Tunisia, encouraged by the entrance of Iran into the Organization for Economic Cooperation and Development and other institutions of the developed powers, are pushing for similar treatment. Two states—Algeria and Nigeria—have been trying to range the countries of Africa behind them in somewhat different approaches: Algeria, stressing ideology and status, demands that a "true representative" of the disinherited continent find its place among the "concert of great powers." Nigeria presses for common fronts on concrete projects like ECOWAS and for a successor to the Lomé Conventions. But neither effort has been disruptive of the more detailed incremental advances made to compensate the poorer states and facilitate the development of the richer ones.

## EVENTFUL SCENARIO

Zimbabwe achieves its independence before the end of the 1970s through a bitter guerrilla war that tears alliances apart and polarizes political relations on all levels. No one is on the side of the Rhodesians initially, but Western efforts to limit the bloodshed and to avoid favoring the same side as the Russians soon create a two-sided conflict. A group of young radicals quickly sweeps away the old nationalist leaders and allies with the Mozambicans, while the Angolans and Cubans are pushing guerrilla war in Namibia. The Russians are taking a hard line in the UN on sanctions for South Africa. Since the United States and South Africa have been trying to get concessions out of Rhodesia, the Africans have linked them together and a number of states have broken off relations with the United States.

When Zimbabwe becomes independent, therefore, this is seen merely as the opening act to the final play on southern Africa rather than as a separate case. Nigeria has ended oil shipments to the United States because the United States is believed to be supporting South Africa. Algeria and Libya have done likewise, and the African states are putting heavy pressure on OPEC to reciprocate their earlier support for the Arab states against Israel. By the early 1980s, there is a full-scale war in South Africa, where neighboring states, using Russian arms and African soldiers, are sustaining heavy losses in that hard-fighting but beleaguered country. Although Britain and the United States have paralyzed the Security Council with their vetoes, Russia and the African states have taken over the UN machinery through the General Assembly, branded South Africa an aggressor, and legitimized their war with the stamp of the UN. When the Nigerian civilian government, mired in corruption and immobilism, is overthrown by a junior officers' coup, the new rulers throw the army into the struggle, marching through Namibia with Russian arms, while Tanzanian soldiers attack from Mozambique with

Chinese arms. This war goes on for a number of years, the South Africans losing half their territory but still holding on to the Rand and to Cape Province. West Germany has kept South Africa supplied with arms; and the United States, trying to avoid a massacre of the whites and achieve a negotiated settlement, has succeeded only in being associated with South Africa in world opinion.

Détente suffers. Although official contacts between the United States and the Soviet Union have been maintained, arms agreements and grains sales have been suspended. The Russians are keeping up the pressure on other trouble spots, such as the Mideast and Southeast Asia; thus the West is unable to focus on or develop a common strategy toward either Russia or Africa.

The South African war finally ends, in 1988, in an exhausted stalemate and partition. There are provisions for negotiations and cooperation between the two resulting states, but they are never able to break through the residue of hostility during the decade. As a result, they maintain an artificial separation and prolong their wartime exhaustion. New gold mines are located in both states, and the black state receives international aid.

War has torn two other corners of the continent, leaving participants shattered and exhausted. Morocco and Algeria went to war over the Western Sahara; as a result of the final stalemate, the Boumedienne regime survived only through a bitter increase in authoritarianism, King Hassan was overthrown by a military coup that could hold the country together only by repression, Mauritania underwent its military coup as well, and the Sahraoui Republic led a precarious existence. In the Horn of Africa, Somalia conquered Ogaden and then Djibouti and in the late 1980s was putting increased pressure on Kenya, but was no better off as a result. The Eritrean Republic underwent a series of internal struggles for leadership, and the revolution in a reduced Ethiopia continued to eat its children.

Like the Congolese and Algerian wars, the three African wars of the 1980s dominate events on the continent as long as they last, and leave scars thereafter. Although it might be thought that in the South African struggle at least Africa would be united, important differences of tactics and commitment separate the moderates from the radicals. Governments in Ghana, Zambia, Nigeria, and Malawi are overthrown on the issue. Subregions—particularly West, Equatorial, and East Africa—split into opposing camps, publicly attacking their neighbors and privately subverting them, Subregional economic cooperation groups break up. Nigeria, Algeria, and Angola, vying for continental leadership, each use the issue to beat the others' radical slogans for action, so that even among the activists there is no unity.

But the three African leaders are not rich enough to supply the needs of the smaller, poorer states, a number of which cluster about the more moderate group of Senegal, the Ivory Coast, Cameroon, and Kenya. This group continues to maintain better relations with the West and to be subject to greater foreign penetration than the more visible leaders. However, the greater foreign presence provides a corrupting element in even these countries, and the resulting increased wealth flows only upward and outward, causing dissatisfaction and unrest at the lower levels of society. Toward the end of their rule, in the early 1980s, the "George Washington" figures in each of these four countries lose their touch, and their entourages devote more time to defending their positions and guarding their nest eggs than promoting genuine development. When the old leaders die there is an interregnum of unpopular control by the entourages, and the military comes to power in each in the middle 1980s. The military first seeks to achieve a degree of redistribution while above all restoring order, but when the first measure frightens foreign investment (because of nationalizations) more than the second assures it, the military changes its policies to a defense (and sharing) of the items of privilege that remain. Growth rates drop, force is needed to keep order, and further military coups ensue—putting in motion the same process of reducing and then protecting privilege. In the process, radical opposition groups spring up among exiles in neighboring countries, and relations between the states involved deteriorate.

The OAU, which has already been reduced to a forum for vague principles by the three African wars, is now being torn to pieces by the continental leadership rivalries. As a result, its ability to resolve minor irritations between member states is

117

disappearing at the time when such irritations are increasing. As long as the war was going on, these disputes were only verbal, but now that the armies have returned home and the incomplete and exhausting nature of the victory has become evident, irritations are erupting in more concrete forms: subversion, support of exile opposition, border claims, border incidents, mobilization of national armies. Instead of mediating, the rival leadership states are seeking to ensure that their allies prevail, and when one side in a dispute seems on the point of doing so, the other seeks support outside the continent. Although the West is scarcely in favor on the continent because of the South African war, some states are finding its members acceptable allies in time of trouble and their opponents are protesting ideologically.

As quarreling breaks out everywhere, economies stagnate and authoritarian regimes multiply, since they are best suited to defending scarce and slowly expanding resources from external attack, putting the lid on internal demand, and maintaining a constant state of military readiness. Paradoxically, the general postwar exhaustion and unproductiveness that have produced this situation prevent the limited hostilities from becoming widespread conflict; there is simply not enough tinder to make brushfires a forest fire. As the 1980s draw to an end, the external world decides that Africa is not worth the conquest, and a tacit hands-off agreement is reached, leaving the continent a ghetto to fight its own battles.

## THE DIFFERENCES

Admittedly, these two scenarios are "stacked," since there is probably general agreement on the desirability of one over the other. In the abstract, there is no guarantee that an "eventful" scenario will turn out badly for the continent and an "uneventful" one turn out well or at least relatively better. Nonetheless, the present contention is that each of these scenarios has a realistic logic of its own that makes such outcomes most likely. As stated earlier, reality read as history in 1990 is most likely to contain parts of both scenarios plus a number of pivotal unforeseen events.

As the future is considered from 1978, however, there are a few discrete events offering policy opportunities that do make a difference between the two outcomes. A negotiated independence for Zimbabwe, encouragement of all opportunities for change in South Africa, expanded subregional cooperation, a new agricultural self-sufficiency, continuing educational growth, continual expansion of the modernized elite, and a problem-solving approach to North-South issues are clearly matters of importance, requiring consideration in external—as well as internal—policy making and providing an opportunity for concerned nations to make a useful contribution to African development and world stability. While a consideration of the policies to be followed for each of these goals would require a separate study, the purpose here has been to show the context and components that are likely to predominate when policy making takes place.

# Africa in the Changing World Economy

Steven Langdon and Lynn K. Mytelka

# Introduction

As Africa heads into the 1980s, new patterns of change are evident throughout the continent. Regimes are being established which break more clearly with the colonial experience, policies are being adopted which emphasize economic independence, and development strategies are taking shape that aim to restructure African relations with the international capitalist economy. This study traces the roots of such changes. In so doing it examines why the postcolonial growth strategies of the 1960s and early 1970s proved inadequate and points out the problems involved in certain of the restructuring options African countries are currently exploring. The study suggests that a set of social and economic forces already apparent in the African environment is pushing many African countries toward self-reliant development strategies, and it explores the directions such options might best take.

In orienting this study we begin from certain notions of development and a political economy approach that emphasize historical processes, international dependency relationships, and class analysis. In this introduction we outline this perspective and preview the structure of the essay as a whole.

It is widely accepted today that the notion of development employed in the 1950s and 1960s—a notion that focused essentially on increases in per capita income averages—was inadequate to the task of evaluating the consequences of the pattern of growth observed. Indeed, such a focus ignored the extent to which certain forms of income growth could *increase* inequalities, *decrease* employment opportunities, and reinforce mass poverty in poorer countries.[1] Clearly, a new concept of development was needed, one that put the main emphasis on reducing poverty, expanding employment, and moving toward greater socioeconomic equality.

*Development*, then, can be thought of as a process of structural change and capital accumulation that moves a society closer to conditions in which the basic needs of people (for shelter, food, clothing, etc.) are met, full employment prevails, and socioeconomic equality is increasing. *Underdevelopment*, in turn, can be thought of as a process of structural change and capital accumulation that moves a society in a direction that makes it more difficult to achieve these conditions. Underdevelopment in this sense can involve significant increases in per capita incomes, but in a form that concentrates gains among a well-off minority and imposes social costs on a poor majority. Underdevelopment is, thus, different from stagnation.

What factors are likely to shape a growth process so as to generate underdevelopment as opposed to development? The analysis that follows starts from two basic assumptions. First, it rejects the notion that economic factors alone will be determinant in such a context. A political economy framework for investigation is likely to be far more valid, in that it recognizes the complex intermeshing of so-called political, economic, and social factors that a process of broad social change involves. Second, it suggests that one cannot isolate the process of change in any given Third World country from that occurring in the world economy as a whole. This is especially true in view of the

[1]Dudley Seers, "What Are We Trying to Measure?" *Journal of Development Studies*, vol. 8, no. 3, April 1972. For a broader treatment, see Mahhub Ul Haq, *The Poverty Curtain*, Columbia University Press, New York, 1976; Irma Adelman and Cynthia T. Morris, *Economic Growth and Social Equity in Developing Countries*, Stanford University Press, Stanford, Calif., 1973; Charles Elliot, *Patterns of Poverty in the Third World*, Praeger, New York, 1975; Paul Streeten, *The Frontiers of Development Study*, Wiley, New York, 1972; and Hollis Chenery et al., *Redistribution With Growth*, Oxford University Press, New York, 1974.

external economic and social penetration that characterized the recent history of most such countries. A world system of economic relationships emerged as early as the seventeenth or eighteenth century. This commercial integration introduced external links and relationships into "periphery" countries with the result that such regions would face a qualitatively different external environment in their internal process of change than the metropolitan European countries had experienced. An appropriate framework in which to analyze the significance of such external ties is provided by Latin American and Caribbean scholars in studies of the political economy of dependence.[2]

The historical evolution of socioeconomic institutions is at the root of a political economy approach to dependence. It is clear that differing regions of the world were incorporated into an international division of labor at different periods and under different conditions. As a result different *institutions* were established and differing *modes of production*[3] emerged in the various periphery areas: slavery in the Caribbean, a curious feudalism in much of Latin America, peasant agriculture in large parts of Africa. The socio-institutional *legacies* of these different patterns of incorporation shape periphery political economies even as ongoing external relationships change. Thus the residue of feudal-type export production under mercantilism is seen as shaping Latin America's subsequent links with the international econ-

[2]The framework sketched below builds upon the work of Theotonio Dos Santos, Celso Furtado, Norman Girvan, and Osvaldo Sunkel.

[3]"A mode of production is defined here by the specific manner in which material surplus is produced and appropriated. For example, Marx defined the capitalist mode of production as one where economic surplus is created by wage laborers and appropriated as surplus value by non-producers who control the means of production . . . most societies . . . are composed of more than one mode of production. But in most societies, one mode of production dominates the others." By domination we mean that "it subjects the functioning of other modes of production to the requirements of its own reproduction." Emmanuel Terray, "Classes and Class Consciousness in the Abron Kingdom of Gyaman," in Maurice Block (ed.), *Marxist Analysis and Social Anthropology*, Wiley, New York, 1975, pp. 90–91, as cited in Ellen K. Trimberger, "State Power and Modes of Production: Implications of the Japanese Transition to Capitalism," *Insurgent Sociologist*, vol. 7, no. 2, Spring 1977, p. 85.

omy. It generated dualism in the periphery, where only a minority moved into more productive capitalist relations and most remained with little or no capitalist relations; and the duality in turn limited the dynamism of those capitalist relations (by restricting market size, for instance). Similarly, the Caribbean's plantation/slavery legacy restricted internal consumer demand and checked the dynamism of subsequent peasant agricultural expansion (because of plantation-land monopolization) even after slavery was abolished.[4]

A second element in this political economy of dependence is the ongoing impact of external links on *internal social relations* in periphery countries. Powerful external ties shape the internal dominance in Third World countries of social classes that are dependent on those ties for their prosperity and their political power. This may occur either directly through control of trade relations based around those ties or indirectly in a more comprehensive technological and ideological sense. This process can be termed *transnational integration*, by which certain periphery social groups are drawn more fully into the dynamic core of the international capitalist economy, thereby benefiting from the growth generated by these links. The result, however, is growing polarization in periphery countries between that integrated minority and the majority of people, who remain segmented in parts of the society dominated by noncapitalist modes of production or in areas of marginal capitalist production relations. For the latter, capital accumulation becomes increasingly more difficult as they face the competitive thrust of technology-intensive firms within the transnational segment.[5]

A third element in a political economy of dependence is the

[4]Norman Girvan, "The Development of Dependency Economics in the Caribbean and Latin America: Review and Comparison," *Social and Economic Studies*, vol. 22, no. 1, March 1973, pp. 1–33.

[5]Osvaldo Sunkel, "Transnational Capitalism and National Disintegration in Latin America," *Social and Economic Studies*, vol. 22, no. 1, March 1973, pp. 132–176; and Theotonio Dos Santos, "The Crisis of Development Theory and the Problem of Dependence in Latin America," in H. Bernstein (ed.), *Underdevelopment and Development*, Penguin Books, London, 1973, pp. 57–80.

set of constraints conducive to continuity. When a political economy is structured around certain forms of external relationships, the costs of transition to new internal structures that collide with these external ties can be very high in the short run. The need to absorb these high short-run costs is likely to breed political dissatisfaction among potentially powerful political groups in the society and generate tensions that potentially could result in the overthrow of existing regimes. It is the fear of such costs as well as the benefits derivable by some from transnational integration that incline governments toward the maintenance of existing external ties, though some adjustments in these may still take place.

These three elements can be combined in an analytical framework that proves useful in examining recent and ongoing change in Africa. The focus of the analysis is on the external pressures and ties created for periphery African societies by the expansion and adjustment of the capitalist world economy. These pressures and ties, it is argued, have generated certain socio-institutional effects that influence contemporary change. Furthermore, such ties in the contemporary context influence both internal class structure and class consciousness within Africa. And finally, such external realities constitute a continuing constraint on rapid transition to new internal structures, even in cases where regimes emerge with some independence from transnational integration and some commitment to escape from historical legacies.

The fundamental argument then is that the structural change and capital accumulation taking place in interrelationship with these strong external links have led and are leading to increasing segmentation and inequality in many African countries, to growing employment problems, and to ongoing poverty for most Africans. The purpose of this article is to examine the dynamics of this process and some of the strategy options open to African countries—and thus to assess the prospects for development within the sub-Saharan part of that continent.

In Chapters 1 and 2 we consider the historical shaping of African political economies and discuss the decolonization process. In Chapter 3 we examine the difficulties and contradictions of the postcolonial economic experience of black Africa, sug-

127

gesting why many countries there have been pushed to explore new options in the contemporary context. In Chapter 4 we critically review certain of these options, suggesting their developmental limitations. Finally, in the conclusion, we explore the self-reliant strategies toward which we believe the change process traced in this essay will take many African countries in the 1980s.

# ONE

# Shaping the African Political Economy

Over the course of five centuries, African economies were shaped by their contact with the expanding, commercialized economies of Europe and North America. The latter countries sought slaves, palm oil, cotton, coffee, copper, and other raw materials, and Africa was induced to supply these by coercion (direct colonial rule, taxation policies, military or police action) or by the penetration of international market-price relations. Africa was drawn into an essentially extractive role in the international division of labor. In this section we trace the mechanisms and consequences of this process.

From the outset European contact with Africa was motivated by a desire to open that continent to direct trade with Europe and its possessions. Gold, ivory, and other luxury goods, formerly exported northward across the Sahara, were among the earlier commodities in the new coastal trade. Although the Portuguese did not establish their first coastal trading fortress until 1482, by the beginning of the sixteenth century gold from the Elmina fortress accounted for approximately one-tenth of the total world supply of gold at that time.[6] Nevertheless, until the Ashanti were subjugated by the British in a series of wars during the nineteenth century, Europeans never controlled the supply of gold or its production.

[6]Edward W. Bovill, *Golden Trade of the Moors*, 2d ed., Oxford University Press, London, 1970, p. 117.

With the discovery of gold in Brazil, European interest in African gold waned. Simultaneously, however, the demand for labor in the New World was rising. Slaves became Africa's first major staple export. By the end of the seventeenth century, three-fifths of the income of the Royal African Company, the leading trading company of the period, came from the slave trade.[7]

The consequences of the slave trade are important to outline, even if they cannot be detailed here, because it is with the slave trade that we see emerging several of the key features that mark present patterns of African underdevelopment.

First, the slave trade initiated the creation of an open exchange economy in Africa by fostering reliance upon a single staple export. As centers of wealth and power developed around the trade in slaves, abolition of the slave trade would trigger the search for new staples and the reaffirmation of external trading ties rather than the development of products for local or regional markets. Second, the slave trade encouraged the growth of coastal towns, thereby accelerating the decline of Sahelian commercial centers, the breakdown of intra-African trading ties, and the reorientation of commercial activity toward coastal centers and from there to Europe. By the end of the eighteenth century a French traveler reported that there remained only one caravan every two or three years along the main western Sahara route.[8]

Third, slaves were a staple that required little diversification of existing methods of production, no significant additional commercialization of factors, and hence no incentive to innovate. These characteristics of the slave as a commodity, the massive hemorrhage of population that further reduced the size of African markets, and the concentration of wealth that resulted from the small number of persons who controlled the trade in slaves combined to distort the process of technological and economic change in Africa. The satisfaction of elite tastes through imports of con-

[7]Anthony G. Hopkins, *An Economic History of West Africa*, Longman Group Ltd., London, 1973, p. 91.
[8]Basil Davidson, *A History of West Africa in the Nineteenth Century*, Anchor Books, Garden City, N.Y., 1966, p. 209.

sumer goods was substituted for the generation of local technology in the service of domestic production—a pattern that persists in contemporary Africa. In the process, established iron-working, salt, and textile industries were ruined. The slave trade thus created a disincentive to the production and export of other commodities.

Fourth, the wealth and power of this slave-trading elite was maintained through its contact with European trading interests. Indeed, the vulnerability of these elites, which derived from their dependence on European weaponry, would later permit the European states to play off competitors for political power and ultimately to colonize these coastal kingdoms. The intrusion of British authority became increasingly evident when, after abolition of the slave trade in 1807, the British sought to enforce this ban in the 1840s and 1850s by demanding the right to seize slave ships in African ports.

In sum, during the period of slavery, the export sector in West Africa constituted a classic enclave activity with few backward or forward linkages to the rest of the economy. What impact it did have on the distribution of incomes, employment, and entrepreneurship was highly negative. The elites that rose during this period, moreover, owed their wealth and power to their association with European trading interests and could not be expected, therefore, to take initiatives in production and trade beyond those stimulated by European demand.

As the slave trade declined in West Africa, it rose in the East. Throughout the eighteenth century the Kamba and Nyika had dominated the inland trading routes in ivory and hides, with export of these to Europe, India, and America mediated at the coast by Mombasa-based Swahili traders. In addition to serving as agents in the interior trade of chains, snuffboxes, and firearms for ivory and hides, the Kamba were also able to produce and market a variety of indigenous trade items to peoples in the interior. Kamba arrow poisons, iron ore smelted by Kamba smiths and fashioned into ornamental chains, game meat, ferrous sand, tobacco, beeswax, bark bags, and foodstuffs figured heavily in domestic exchange.

Penetration of inland markets by Swahili coastal traders began as ivory-producing regions near the coast were denuded of elephants and, more important, the demand for slaves rose. The growth of a plantation economy in the French-dominated islands of Mauritius and Réunion and the development of clove production by the Omani Arabs of Zanzibar and Pemba both stimulated the demand for East African slaves. By 1810 some 8,000 slaves were being sold annually at Kilwa and Zanzibar, and although French demand slackened as a result of British abolitionist pressures, Zanzabari demand continued to rise well into the 1860s, when it was estimated that some 45,000 slaves were sold annually in the Zanzibar market.[9] Only with the Anglo-Zanzibar treaty of 1873 did the trade in East African slaves diminish to a trickle.

As in West Africa, abolition of the slave trade in East Africa made possible the reemergence of "legitimate" commerce. This time, however, it would not be a trade based on luxury goods but a trade in inputs essential to the European industrialization process then under way.

In West Africa, palm and later groundnut production replaced slaves as a staple export. This change responded to the rising European demand for oils as an input in the soap industry and as a lubricant for machinery. The physical properties of this new staple made possible the emergence of a new class of commodity-producing peasants whose production was geared to the export market. It could be produced efficiently on a small scale by households possessing little capital, employing family labor, and using traditional tools. The shift to palm and groundnut production increased the number of producers incorporated into the emerging international division of labor and marked the confirmation of an open exchange economy in Africa.

The increased commercialization of land and labor during the nineteenth century, moreover, stimulated a pattern of migration from the interior—contemporary Mali, Upper Volta, Rwanda, Burundi, Malawi—to centers of mineral and agricultural pro-

[9]Edward A. Alpers, "The Nineteenth Century: Prelude to Colonialism," in B. A. Ogot and J. A. Kieran (eds.), *Zamani: A Survey of East African History*, Longman Inc., New York, 1968.

duction. While the *mise en valeur* of coastal trading centers, mineral-producing areas, and major regions of export-oriented agricultural production accelerated, the African interior was consigned to the role of a reserve whose principal staple export increasingly became labor.

Palm and groundnut production, however, provided little opportunity for the average peasant to accumulate capital and almost no incentive for technological innovation or the use of machinery. As palm and groundnut production was dependent upon the level of demand in Europe for oils, expansion or contraction of this economic activity was tied to periods of growth and depression in Europe. When the European depressions of 1862–1866 and 1886–1890 caused a fall in prices, and new techniques to increase productivity were not available, African incomes from palm and groundnut production began to fall and production was cut back.

It was during this period that farmers in the Gold Coast spontaneously and successfully initiated cocoa production as an alternative. Cocoa exports amounted to 34.5 percent of the value of Gold Coast exports by 1910 and by 1915 had reached 64 percent, replacing palm oil and kernels, which since 1886 had constituted 50 percent of exports.[10] Elsewhere, the European desire to commercialize production in Africa led to new exercises in the application of colonial rule as the Congress of Berlin in 1885 had made physical occupation the sine qua non of territorial sovereignty and hence a prerequisite to further commercialization.

---

[10]Geoffrey Kay, *The Political Economy of Colonialism in Ghana*, Cambridge University Press, New York, 1972, p. 334.

# TWO

# The Colonial Political Economy

Despite variations in the mode of production that became dominant under colonialism, colonial rule would everywhere confirm the essentially extractive role for Africa in the international division of labor, promote surplus drainage to make domestic capital accumulation difficult, entrench the monopoly character of domestic production, and promote the emergence of new social strata. In so doing colonialism would, by shaping African political economies, render substantial change in the immediate post-independence period extremely difficult. Indeed, those who acceded to positions of power at independence in most former French, Belgian, and British colonies were ideal partners in a postindependence symbiotic relationship with international capital.

## COMMODITY PRODUCTION

Since substitutes for palm and groundnut oil were abundant, the immediate preoccupation of colonial states was the search for new staple exports, reflecting both the economic needs of metropolitan economic actors and the needs of the colonial state for a tax base. While Nigeria remained West Africa's principal exporter of palm products, British, French, Belgian, and German colonial states, the settlers in Kenya and Zambia and those who located in Rhodesia, the private companies that directly admin-

135

istered Zambia and Zaire,[11] and the concessionary companies created by France to commercialize production in Equatorial Africa set about promoting new exportable commodities. Peasants in Mali, Upper Volta, Nigeria, and Uganda were induced to grow cotton and cocoa; sisal plantations were established in Tanzania; coffee estates were created in Kenya and the Ivory Coast; wood was extracted in Gabon; and gold, copper, manganese, tin, iron, diamonds, and uranium were mined in Zambia, Zaire, the People's Republic of the Congo, Mauritania, Ghana, and the Central African Empire. The largest and most concerted effort in the pre–World War I period, however, was expended in the attempt to grow cotton.

Textile production was the backbone of the first industrial revolution in Europe. Growth of this industry was, however, dependent upon imports of raw cotton from the United States. The American Civil War and the subsequent development of textile production in the United States created a cotton famine and strongly motivated the ensuing alliance between colonial states and textile manufacturers.

In 1902 the British Cotton Growing Association and the German Kolonialwirtschaftliches Komitee were formed to promote cotton production in Tanzania. By 1912 the value of cotton exported from that country amounted to nearly $500,000.[12] In 1899 territorial concessionary companies were established in Equatorial Africa for the purpose of developing and exploiting industrial export crops, principal among which was cotton. By 1950 the French Federation of Equatorial Africa supplied over 80 percent of total cotton production in the French colonies. It met approximately 11 percent of France's needs in raw cotton and saved France $30 million annually that would otherwise have had to be spent for purchases in the dollar zone. At least 1.5 million Africans, or approximately two-thirds of the adult pop-

[11]As many African countries have changed names several times since 1900, for simplicity and clarity we will refer to them by the most contemporary of these names.

[12]This figure is cited in Kenneth Ingham, *A History of East Africa*, Praeger, New York, pp. 195–196, as 2.1 million marks.

ulation of the Central African Empire and Chad, were by that time wholly or partly dependent upon cotton sales to supply their cash income.[13] Research and development activities undertaken by institutes financed by the French state were intended to support tropical-plantation-agriculture crops for export to France. Thus the first such institutes to be established in the 1940s—the Institut de Recherches pour les Huiles et Oléagineaux and the Institut de Recherches du Coton and des Textiles Exotiques— worked with private companies such as the Compagnie Française pour le Développement des Fibres Textiles (CFDT), entrusted by the colonial state to commercialize tropical production. Cotton production rose dramatically in West Africa and rivaled groundnuts as a principal export.[14] More important, concentration on cotton production, with the peculiar demands it places upon the soil, accompanied by decreased attention to food crops, led to a decline in food production.[15] A breakdown in complementary farmer-herder watering and fertilization patterns resulted from both increasing herd size and land-use patterns; this reduced the adaptability of Sahelian populations to the climatic changes that intervened in the late 1960s and early 1970s, and exacerbated the ensuing famine.

The plantation system in Tanzania left other legacies with negative consequences for the future development of that political economy. Because of the low wages offered on sisal and other plantations, wage workers were obliged to maintain the security afforded by their membership in rural-based kinship groups. Labor thus remained largely migratory. The planters

---

[13]Richard Adloff and Virginia Thompson, *The Emerging States of French Equatorial Africa*, Stanford University Press, Stanford, Calif., 1960, p. 174.

[14]Malian cotton exports, for example, rose from 7 percent of total exports in 1959 to 40 percent by 1968. See Bonnie Campbell, "Neocolonialism, Economic Dependence and Political Change: A Case Study of Cotton and Textiles Production in the Ivory Coast, 1960 to 1970," *Review of African Political Economy*, no. 2, 1975, pp. 36–53.

[15]Dharam Ghai estimates that in much of Africa food production did not increase during the 1960s by more than 1.5 percent per year, with the consequence that food production per capita fell. See Ghai, "Perspectives on Future Economic Prospects and Problems in Africa," in Jagdish N. Bhagwati (ed.), *Economics and World Order*, Free Press, New York, 1972, pp. 257–286.

were unable to get permanent workers, which led to the substitution of capital for labor and allowed the planters to reduce employment. This situation also served to perpetrate the unskilled character of the Tanzanian labor force which endures today.[16]

Finally, the difference between a settler colony, such as Kenya became, and a colony with an economy based upon peasant production, as in Uganda, is apparent from a comparison of production, employment, and export figures. By 1937 the volume of Uganda's exports was almost twice that of Kenya's. Of these exports, moreover, 80 percent derived from African agriculture, mainly cotton, while not more than 15 percent of Kenya's exports came from African production and more than half of these came from the export of hides.[17] In contrast to the petty-commodity producers who dominated production in Uganda, Europeans settled in Kenya, encouraged by colonial policy, in order to provide sufficient traffic on the railroad from Mombasa to the cotton-producing areas of Uganda. To utilize the large tracts of land they received in the former Kikuyu highlands, Europeans permitted Kikuyu "squatters" to farm their lands for a fee or employed Kikuyu whose land holdings, limited by colonial policy to reserves, were insufficient to provide income for subsistence and taxes. In the mid-1920s more than half the able-bodied Kikuyu and neighboring Luo were working for Europeans. African exports, which up to 1912 had constituted 70 percent of all exports, by 1928 accounted for less than 20 percent, and from 1925 the absolute value of African export production declined as the "reserves" increasingly relapsed into subsistence farming to support their growing populations and to maintain those whose earnings from wage labor on the European farms were below the subsistence level.[18] Exploitation of Kikuyu farm labor and dep-

[16]Justinian Rweyemamu, *Underdevelopment and Industrialization in Tanzania: A Study of Perverse Capitalist Industrial Development*, Oxford University Press, New York, 1974, p. 23.

[17]Bethwell A. Ogot, "Kenya under the British, 1895 to 1963," in Ogot and Kieran (eds.), *Zamani*, p. 274.

[18]Colin Leys, *Underdevelopment in Kenya*, University of California Press, Berkeley, 1975, p. 32.

rivation of their land would ultimately drive the Kikuyu into open revolt in what became known as the Mau Mau rebellion.

## THE MECHANISMS OF SURPLUS APPROPRIATION

Thus agricultural and mineral production and exports grew. But the increased surplus generated by such activities did not lead to substantial capital accumulation among Africans in the colonies, even when a large part of the production was concentrated in African hands. The reasons are many.

First, colonies were expected to be self-supporting. This implied that they would have to pay their own administrative costs. Where individual colonies were unable to balance their own budgets, associations were formed with wealthier colonies, such as the French Federation of West Africa, the French Federation of Equatorial Africa, and the East African Customs Union, through which surplus could be transferred. Not until the late 1940s would the colonial powers undertake substantial direct transfers of funds to their colonies. Even then funds allocated under the French Fonds d'investissements pour le Développement économique et sociale, established in 1946, went exclusively to nonproductive ventures such as infrastructure—especially administrative buildings and airports that saddled the postindependence governments with high maintenance costs—or to geological surveys and agricultural export production that furthered the extroverted character of the colonial economies. The absence of any allocation to industrial development prolonged the bias toward primary production in these economies.

Second, growing out of the policy that colonies must be self-supporting, the structure of colonial budgets revealed that the largest single expenditure was for expatriate salaries and, later, pensions. Recurrent expenditures averaged 63 percent of the Ghanaian budget in the period 1900–1929. Public-sector wages represented 46 percent of total budgetary expenditures in Senegal as late as the 1950s.[19] Little remained in colonial budgets for

[19]Kay, *Colonialism in Ghana*, p. 27; and Theresa Hayter, *French Aid*, Overseas Development Institute, London, 1966, p. 40.

housing, health, sanitation, or education, and what did was distributed largely for the benefit of the expatriate community in the colonies, even though a proportionally heavier tax burden fell upon the African native population.

Lines of rail passed through areas of European settlement (Kenya and Zambia) or serviced expatriate-owned mines (western Ghana) as opposed to African-owned cocoa farms (southeastern Ghana). Roads, hospitals, sanitation systems, power lines, and schools were built in areas of expatriate residence to the exclusion of urban African townships and rural areas. Additional levies were required of African populations to repair roads and maintain schools in areas of African residence while general revenues provided the same services in European areas. European businesses, moreover, benefited from privileged access to profitable markets through tariff protection and subsidized rail rates to the detriment of their African competitors.

Third, the creation of monopolies also served to direct capital accumulation away from Africans and permit its appropriation by expatriate interests. Monopolies on the most profitable export crops (coffee in Kenya) or key inputs such as the best agricultural land (the Kenyan "white highlands") or an adequate supply of cheap agricultural labor (through the *corvée* system in Senegal, the Ivory Coast, and other French and Belgian territories) were created and maintained by the colonial state. Licensing was also used to eliminate African competitors, as in the competition of African road transportation with the railroads that serviced expatriate mines and farms.

Monopolies created by private European companies were sanctioned by the colonial state. Such monopolies permitted price fixing in the export trade [where three expatriate firms, the United Africa Company (UAC), Compagnie Française de L'Afrique Occidentale (CFAO), and SCOA, handled two-thirds of West Africa's trade], in shipping (Elder Dempster for the British colonies; Chargeurs Reunis and Fabre et Fraissinet for the French), or in the purchase of cocoa (the Cocoa Pool of 1937 in Ghana) and cotton (the operations of the CFDT in French West Africa). The unequal exchange that resulted between monopsonistic, expatriate purchasers and shippers and small African producers severely limited the extent to which the latter could accumulate capital. Unequal access to credit and a monopoly of commercial credit in the hands of only a few expatriate banks affected the ability of African farmers and entrepreneurs to expand production, generate surplus, accumulate capital, and invest in forward-linking enterprises.

Marketing boards were also used to regulate African agriculture and enable the appropriation of surplus. The Cocoa Marketing Board in Ghana is a good example. With a monopoly on the purchase of cocoa from producers, the Cocoa Marketing Board was able to set prices below world-market prices, thereby accumulating surplus in good times and maintaining a stable income for cocoa farmers when world-market prices fell. In theory the Cocoa Marketing Board encouraged production by stabilizing prices for the producers. In practice, between 1947 and 1961 cocoa farmers received an annual average of only 54.7 percent of the export price of cocoa. As a consequence the Cocoa Marketing Board accumulated huge surplusses: $148,000,000 by 1958. These surplusses were invested in long-term British government securities at low rates of interest.[20] In effect, the colonies thus lent money to Britain for its postwar recovery.

In addition to serving as mechanisms for the transfer of surplus from Africa to the European metropoles, the Currency Boards, established by the British in East and West Africa and by the French in West and Equatorial Africa, stabilized exchange rates and facilitated trade and investment flows between the metropole and colony. They also indirectly determined the money supplies of the African countries, thus controlling the foreign-exchange reserves and domestic credit policies of the Africans.

It should be pointed out that whereas most former British colonies had initiated policies to "close" their economies by bringing monetary policy within the ambit of national institutions during the 1960s, the former French colonies of West and Equatorial Africa continue to maintain close ties to the French Central

---

[20]F. Bourret, *Ghana: The Road to Independence*, Stanford University Press, Stanford, Calif., 1960, p. 204; and Tony Killick, "The Economics of Cocoa," in W. Birmingham, I. Neustadt, and E. N. Omaboe (eds.), *A Study of Contemporary Ghana*, vol. 1, Allen and Unwin, London, 1966.

Bank. Indeed, it was not until 1972 that the Administrative Council of the Banque des États de l'Afrique Centrale had an African majority.

## INDUSTRIAL GROWTH

Not only did increased agricultural and mineral production and export not serve as the basis for capital accumulation in Africa, but throughout much of the colonial period, by actively discouraging both processing activities and manufacturing in the colonies, the colonial state reduced domestic linkages within its colonies, further segmenting the political economy. Thus the French prohibited oil processing in Senegal in the nineteenth century. But they were not alone in fostering an international division of labor that reserved manufacturing activities to the center and relegated the periphery to the task of supplying raw materials and agricultural products. To this end, when necessary, British colonial policy actively thwarted attempts at forward-linking activities. When United Kingdom twine manufacturers balked, for example, at the possible competition from British sisal producers in Tanzania who had begun to manufacture twine, the British government obliged the Tanzanian company to negotiate with the U.K. federation. Once having agreed to allow the U.K. federation to determine the price of its product in that country, the industry did not survive for long.[21]

By 1949 most industry in Africa was limited to simple ginning, milling, and decorticating activities. In the Congo, sugar refining only began in 1938. In Cameroon, saw-milling began in 1944. Oil and soap manufacture from imported caustic soda, using local palm oil in the Ivory Coast and coconut oil in Tanzania, only began in the 1930s. In each case, moreover, processing activities were largely in non-African hands: Europeans in West Africa, Europeans and Asians in East Africa.

During the 1950s the pattern of industrialization in the colonies

[21] E. A. Brett, *Colonialism and Underdevelopment in East Africa: The Politics of Economic Change 1919–1939*, Nok, New York, 1973, pp. 267–275.

shifted, with large European firms beginning to invest in assembly and manufacturing activities geared to the local market. Having penetrated African markets through exports, manufacturers of consumer goods found further imports constrained by balance-of-payments problems and markets narrowed by the imposition of import duties and the operation of monopolistic shipping and trading interests. Moreover, the emerging bourgeoisie during the colonial period was already orientated toward the purchase of European goods and looked with favor upon the interest of European firms in locating plants in Africa. During the 1950s bicycle assembly began in Cameroon; textile production in the Central African Empire and Senegal; breweries in many countries of West and Equatorial Africa; clothing manufacture in Nigeria; and tobacco in Zambia, Tanzania, and the Congo. Much of this industry was in European hands.[22]

## THE SOCIAL STRUCTURE UNDER COLONIALISM

The consequences of the pattern of agricultural and industrial production and ownership that emerged during the colonial period are broadly summarized in Table 1 in terms of a number of income, linkage, infrastructure, and social polarization effects. The table does not, however, reveal the kind of social structure that colonialism generated and that persists into the postindependence period, a social structure that we have argued produced a dominant African stratum whose interests lay in further close association with international capital.

The evolving social structure of periphery African economies did differ considerably with variations in colonial production patterns, as outlined in Table 1. Wide penetration of metropolitan

---

[22]See Rweyemamu, *Underdevelopment and Industrialization in Tanzania*, p. 115; J. O. Odufalu, "Indigenous Enterprise in Nigerian Manufacturing," *Journal of Modern African Studies*, vol. 9, no. 4, December 1971, pp. 597–601; Ann Seidman, "Import-Substitution Industry in Zambia," *Journal of Modern African Studies*, vol. 12, no. 4, December 1974, pp. 601–603; and G. Ngango, *Les Investissements d'Origine extérieure en Afrique francophone*, Presence Africaine, Paris, 1973, p. 286ff.

**TABLE 1**

**A Tentative Typology of Colonial Experiences in Africa**

| Area of Impact | *Nature of Colonial Production* | | | | |
| --- | --- | --- | --- | --- | --- |
| | *Peasant Agricultural Production, e.g., Ghana (cocoa), Uganda (cotton), Senegal (groundnut)* | *Large-Scale Mineral Production, e.g., Zambia, Zaire (copper)* | *Plantation Agricultural Production, e.g., Tanzania (sisal)* | *Settler Economies, e.g., Kenya, Angola* | *Labor Migration Areas, e.g., Upper Volta* |
| *Indigenous income effects* | High, widespread | High, concentrated | Low, widespread | Low, concentrated | Very low |
| *Social polarization effects* | Moderate among Africans and between regions | Very high among Africans and regions | Low among Africans and regions | Very high among races, low among Africans, moderate regionally | Very low among Africans |

| Linkage effects (B: backward; F: forward; FD: final demand) | Moderate B, low F, high FD | Low | Low B and F but moderate FD | Very high, especially F and B | Low |
| Income-fluctuation problems | High | Moderate | Low | Moderate | Quite low |
| Provision of infrastructure: transport, education, health, communications | High, widespread | High but very concentrated | Moderate, concentrated | High, widespread | Very low |

NOTE: Differences in experiences and regimes also depend upon (1) the economic structure of the colonial power (e.g., U.K. vs. Portugal), (2) the particular staple produced (e.g., coffee vs. cotton), and (3) other geographic/climatic features (e.g., land scarcity).

SOURCE: Chart prepared by the authors.

145

capital, for instance, drew subsistence producers together into new commercial relations in peasant agricultural areas; such peasantries thus emerged as important social classes in colonies such as Ghana, Uganda, and Nigeria. In areas of large-scale mineral extraction like Zambia and Zaire, on the other hand, peasants were much less important in the political economy, while urbanized wage workers emerged as a more self-conscious social force. In Tanzania, with its large plantation sector, still other patterns were evident. There, organized rural plantation workers became an important element in the colonial African social structure and in the nationalist reactions against that structure. In a settler economy like Kenya, however, rural squatters (a kind of rural proletariat without access to their own land, as opposed to the migrant workers on Tanzanian plantations) became a critical social class. In interaction with the urban wage-labor force generated by wider settler-spurred infrastructure and industry in Kenya, this rural proletariat ultimately formed the social base for a successful challenge to settler control, a form of colonialism generally much more tenacious than that associated with other production strategies.

Despite these differences in basic social structure, though, one common social phenomenon was evident throughout the African colonies. Everywhere the exchange relations with metropolitan economies and the penetration of metropolitan cultural institutions were spawning the emergence of a new African social class, responding to new economic opportunities in trade and in colonial bureaucracies and associated with the culture of the metropolis. Godfrey Mutiso termed the members of the new class the "asomi": those who "had rejected the institutional framework of traditional society . . . and were to be converted into tools of accelerated societal penetration by the missionaries as Catechists and by administrators as clerks and petty functionaries in colonial society."[23]

This notion nicely captures the cultural and educational as-

[23]Godfrey C. M. Mutiso, "Cleavage and the Organizational Base of Politics in Kenya: A Theoretical Framework," *Journal of Eastern African Research and Development*, vol. 3, no. 1, 1973, pp. 39–64.

similation toward the metropolis that characterized the economic positions into which this group moved. These Africans played roles in trade relations and in state institutions that mediated between the metropolis and the local population. Such mediation required some capacity to manipulate and understand the metropolitan cultural/language infrastructure, yet as clearly required for success some continuing roots in the nonmetropolitan cultures of the periphery. It is important to recognize, though, that the bureaucratic roles that such asomi could assume were necessarily subordinate in a colonized state and that the economic opportunities that were open were essentially marginal and firmly defined by dominant metropolitan economic actors.

The Ghanaian case is one of the most striking testimonies to the restrictions placed on this asomi role. Prior to full colonization, British penetration along the Gold Coast was marked by Africans assuming important roles in commercial trade and filling senior bureaucratic positions in the British administraion. With colonization, however, credit provision became skewed more and more to metropolitan trading companies and Africans found their potential for competition with such firms more and more reduced. They were forced into brokerage roles; their opportunities to accumulate capital diminished and they were increasingly dependent on the expatriate firms for which they worked. The result was that no African bourgeoisie, in the full sense of that term, could emerge; instead, a more restricted petit bourgeoisie of small traders and transport entrepreneurs emerged as a powerful class. Similarly, the color bar prevented Africans from rising to positions of importance in government or the bureaucracy until quite late in the colonial period. The result was again the emergence on the fringes of colonial organization of a petit bourgeoisie of clerks and teachers.

In certain African countries, some chiefs were able to convert their positions of authority in traditional society into prominent economic roles under colonialism—as into rich cocoa farmers in Ghana and plantation owners in the Ivory Coast. Where this happened, it is reasonable to speak of something of a rural African bourgeoisie emerging under colonialism. But such groups, even where they emerged, were generally weaker and less significant in the ongoing social dynamics of colonial change than the petit bourgeois asomi.

The social consciousness and political perspective of this petit bourgeoisie have been brilliantly if scathingly described by Frantz Fanon:

The national bourgeoisie of underdeveloped countries is not engaged in production, nor in invention, nor building, nor labor; it is completely canalized into activities of the intermediary type. Its innermost vocation seems to be to keep in the running and to be part of the racket. The psychology of the national bourgeoisie is that of the businessman, not that of a captain of industry; and it is only too true that the greed of the settlers and the system of embargoes set up by colonialism have hardly left them any other choice. . . .The national middle class discovers its historic mission: that of intermediary. Seen through its eyes, its mission has nothing to do with transforming the nation; it consists, prosaically, of being the transmission line between the nation and a capitalism, rampant though camouflaged, which today puts on the mask of neo-colonialism. The national bourgeoisie will be quite content with the role of the Western bourgeoisie's business agent, and it will play its part without any complexes in a most dignified manner. But this same lucrative role, this cheap-Jack's function, this meanness of outlook and this absence of all ambition symbolize the incapacity of the national middle class to fulfill its historic role of bourgeoisie.[24]

Such a petit bourgeoisie often provided the leadership core of the various African movements against colonialism because, by its nature, colonialism attempted to keep most significant intermediary roles in metropolitan hands. Thus, as Fanon stresses, these African groups would use independence to transfer intermediary roles to their own control. But the shaping of these petit bourgeois elements, through the restricted roles they had been given under colonialism, must be seen as critical to the later incapacity of this class to carry through postcolonial transformations.

Political independence *was* achieved. The contradictions involved in the asomi role, given that colonial color bars and met-

[24]Frantz Fanon, *The Wretched of the Earth*, Grove Press, New York, 1968, pp. 149–153.

ropolitan trading-company domination blocked full assimilation of such asomi, could not be avoided. In Mutiso's terms, a "dissociative asomi" emerged, blocked from full bourgeois advance, and turned back to other elements in African society to help organize and articulate the long-term resentment of colonialism that continued to grow among peasants and wage workers. The costs of maintaining colonial control escalated for the European powers in the face of riots in Ghana and Uganda, revolt in Malagasy, Mau Mau rebellion in Kenya, and strikes and political protest throughout other parts of Africa. At the same time, changing strategies of dominant economic interests in Western Europe eased the transition from formal colonial control. Metropolitan trading companies, for example, were increasingly prepared to move into industrial production in periphery countries, as the United Africa Company did in the early 1950s in West Africa. European industrial firms were showing a willingness and organizational ability to establish foreign manufacturing subsidiaries in colonial territories rather than rely on import markets there. European economic interest in controlling intermediary roles in trade had, in short, decreased considerably.

# THREE

# Postcolonial Africa

Decolonization was *not* irrelevant to African development prospects. The "enforced bilateralism" of colonialism was ended, widening the commercial options of African countries. The petit bourgeois elements that led nationalist movements used their new state power to shift control of intermediary roles to themselves. African economies became increasingly "closed" in their relationship with the international capitalist economy, in the sense that more monetary control rested in the periphery and more trade barriers were erected there. However, the character of the emerging African bourgeoisies, the transitional costs of any strategy to change development patterns significantly, and Western European pressures to maintain past links (with persuasion running the gamut from foreign aid flows to military intervention) all combined to limit the impact of decolonization.

Data from across the continent, summarized in Tables 2–4, show that postcolonial African economies have perpetuated or generated staggering income inequalities and have maintained much of their population in conditions of absolute poverty. These economies, moreover, remain very much oriented around raw material production and export for previous metropolitan markets—France, the U.K., and Belgium—with some diversification of markets to include other European Economic Community (EEC) member states, most notably Germany and the Netherlands. In only 8 of the 35 independent African states has a non-EEC country become the major trading partner of an African country. Similarly, only in Mauritius do we find manufactures among the principal products exported. Social structure has shifted somewhat with the replacement of European intermediaries by an emerging African bourgeoisie, and economic structures have often been modified with some increase in industrial production. But fundamental transformations in social structure or in the African place in the international division of labor were not evident.

Holding power in the postcolonial context has proved to be difficult for independent regimes, however. Coups, counter-coups, and political crises have marked the conflict over state authority that has become widespread across the continent.

On one level, this political instability reflects the inevitable dynamics of asomi-led decolonization. Throughout Africa those segments of the African petit bourgeoisie who led successful nationalist movements attempted in the postindependence period to use their new control over the state to direct financial resources and economic opportunities to themselves, in order to consolidate their economic and social position and become something of a dominant bourgeoisie.[25] Until they could achieve such dominance, though, that segment controlling the state (often united by ethnic ties) was highly vulnerable to attack from other petit bourgeois segments (themselves often ethnically based) who wished to use state resources and regulations to foster *their* embourgeoisement. Petit bourgeois segments with a base in the military were particularly able to launch effective attacks.

Moreover, mass discontent with postcolonial regimes often existed to support such take-overs—primarily because independence had not brought the rapid rises in mass living standards that political leaders had promised. Indeed, popular resistance

[25]For a closer look at this transition, see Roger Murray, "Second Thoughts on Ghana," *New Left Review*, vol. 42, 1967; Ronald Cohen, *Ethnicity, Social Class, and Political Power: With Some Reference to Nigeria*, Faculty of Commerce and Social Science, University of Birmingham, England, Occasional Paper 14, February 1971; Leys, *Underdevelopment in Kenya*; and R. Rathbone, "Businessmen in Politics: Party Struggle in Ghana 1949–1957," *Journal of Development Studies*, vol. 9, no. 3, April 1973, pp. 391–401.

**TABLE 2**

**Income Distribution**

| | Per capita GNP | | National Income Shares | | | Estimate of 1969 Population Below $75/year | |
|---|---|---|---|---|---|---|---|
| | Year | $ U.S. | Lowest 40% | Middle 40% | Top 20% | Millions | % of Pop. |
| Benin (Dahomey) | 1959 | 87 | 15.5 | 34.5 | 50.0 | 2.3 | 90.1 |
| Chad | 1958 | 78 | 18.0 | 39.0 | 43.0 | 2.7 | 77.5 |
| Gabon | 1968 | 497 | 8.8 | 23.7 | 67.5 | 3.1 | 15.5 |
| Ivory Coast | 1970 | 247 | 10.8 | 32.1 | 57.1 | 1.4 | 28.5 |
| Kenya | 1969 | 136 | 10.0 | 22.0 | 68.0 | — | — |
| Madagascar | 1960 | 120 | 13.5 | 25.5 | 61.0 | 4.7 | 69.6 |
| Niger | 1960 | 97 | 18.0 | 40.0 | 42.0 | 2.3 | 59.9 |
| Senegal | 1960 | 245 | 10.0 | 26.0 | 64.0 | 1.3 | 35.3 |
| Sierra Leone | 1968 | 159 | 9.6 | 22.4 | 68.0 | 1.5 | 61.5 |
| Tanzania | 1967 | 89 | 13.0 | 26.0 | 61.0 | 9.3 | 72.9 |
| Uganda | 1970 | 126 | 17.1 | 35.8 | 47.1 | 4.1 | 49.8 |
| Zambia | 1959 | 230 | 14.5 | 28.5 | 57.0 | 0.3 | 7.5 |

SOURCE: Hollis Chenery et al., *Redistribution With Growth*, Oxford University Press, London, 1974, Table I.1, pp. 8–9, and Table I.2, p. 12.

## TABLE 3

### Composition and Direction of Exports, 1961 and 1975

| Country | Product | Composition of Trade | | Partner | Direction of Trade | |
|---|---|---|---|---|---|---|
| | | 1961 (%) | 1975 (%) | | 1961 (%) | 1975 (%) |
| *West Africa* | | | | | | |
| *Benin* | Cotton lint | — | 27 | France | 73 | 53 |
| | Cocoa beans | — | 19 | Nigeria | — | 14 |
| | Palm product | 72 | 15 | Federal Republic of Germany (FRG) | — | 14 |
| | Total | 72 | 61* | | 73 | 81 |
| *Gambia* | Groundnuts, oil, meal, and cake | 93 | 95 | U.K. | 50 | 50 |
| | | | | Netherlands | — | 21 |
| | | | | Italy | — | — |
| | Total | 93† | 95 | | 50 | 71 |
| *Ghana* | Cocoa | 60 | 64 | U.K. | 29 | 15 |
| | Logs | 13 | 11 | U.S. | 23 | 11 |
| | | | | Netherlands | 12 | 10 |
| | Total | 73 | 75‡ | | 64 | 36 |
| *Guinea* | Alumina§ | | 72 | France | 18 | |
| | Pineapples | | 10 | Cameroon§ | 11 | |
| | Coffee | | 6 | U.S.S.R. | 9 | |
| | Total | | 88¶ | | 38 | |
| *Ivory Coast* | Coffee | 43 | 24 | France | 52 | 27 |
| | Cocoa beans | 21 | 19 | U.S. | 14 | 10 |
| | Timber | 18 | 14 | Netherlands | 7 | 10 |
| | Total | 82 | 57 | | 73 | 47 |
| *Liberia* | Iron ore | 57 | 74 | U.S. | 46 | 22 |
| | Rubber | 29 | 12 | Netherlands | 22 | — |
| | Diamonds | 5 | 5 | FRG | — | 21 |
| | Total | 91† | 91 | | 68 | 43 |
| *Mali* | Cotton | 6 | 39 | France | 18 | 23 |
| | Groundnuts | 38 | 15 | Ivory Coast | 25 | 6 |
| | Fish | 23 | 2 | China | — | 29 |
| | Total | 67 | 56 | | 43 | 58 |

154

### TABLE 3 (Continued)

### Composition and Direction of Exports, 1961 and 1975

| Country | Product | Composition of Trade | | Partner | Direction of Trade | |
|---|---|---|---|---|---|---|
| | | 1961 (%) | 1975 (%) | | 1961 (%) | 1975 (%) |
| Mauritania | Iron one | 82 | 68 | France | 32 | 22 |
| Niger | Groundnuts | 67 | 15 | France | 78 | 66 |
| | Uranium | — | 43 | FRG | — | 15 |
| | | | | Nigeria | 16 | — |
| | Total | 67 | 58 | | 94 | 81 |
| Nigeria | Crude petroleum | 7 | 93 | U.K. | 44 | 13 |
| | Cocoa beans | 19 | 4 | U.S. | 11 | 26 |
| | Palm kernels | 11 | — | Netherlands | 13 | 10 |
| | Total | 37 | 97 | | 68 | 49 |
| Senegal | Groundnut oil and cake | 83 | 39 | France | 76 | 47 |
| | Phosphates | 4 | 22 | U.K. | 3 | 8 |
| | Total | 87 | 61 | | 79 | 55 |
| Sierra Leone | Diamonds | 54 | 54 | U.K. | 79 | 52 |
| | Iron ore | 16 | 11 | Netherlands | 9 | 13 |
| | Palm kernels | 8 | 4 | U.S. | — | 12 |
| | Total | 78 | 69 | | 88 | 77 |
| Togo | Phosphates | 3 | 79 | France | 58 | 39 |
| | Cocoa beans | 28 | 12 | Netherlands | 10 | 32 |
| | Coffee | 27 | 4 | FRG | — | 10 |
| | Total | 58 | 92‡ | | 68 | 81 |
| Upper Volta | Live animals | | 36 | Ghana | 76 | — |
| | Hides and skins | | 18 | France | 11 | 29 |
| | Cotton fiber | | 16 | Ivory Coast | 3 | 26 |
| | Total | | 70 | | 90 | 55 |

## TABLE 3 (Continued)
### Composition and Direction of Exports, 1961 and 1975

| | | Composition of Trade | | | Direction of Trade | |
|---|---|---|---|---|---|---|
| | | 1961 | 1975 | | 1961 | 1975 |
| Country | Product | (%) | (%) | Partner | (%) | (%) |
| Central Africa | | | | | | |
| Burundi | Coffee | 87 | 88 | U.S. | | 45 |
| | Cotton | 6 | — | FRG | | 22 |
| | Tea | — | 3 | | | |
| | Total | 93† | 91 | | | 67 |
| Cameroon | Cocoa | 21 | 25 | France | 59 | 27 |
| | Coffee | 17 | 24 | Netherlands | 14 | 22 |
| | Alumina | 17 | — | U.S.S.R. | — | 11 |
| | Total | 55 | 49 | | 73 | 60 |
| Central | Coffee | 29 | 23 | France | 69 | 42 |
| African | Cotton | 45 | 23 | U.S. | 5 | 8 |
| Empire | Diamonds | 11 | 20 | Netherlands | — | 8 |
| | Total | 85 | 66 | | 74 | 58 |
| Chad | Raw cotton | 80 | 63 | France | 76 | 10 |
| | Meat | — | 8 | Nigeria | 8 | 15 |
| | | | | Japan | — | 4 |
| | Total | 80 | 71 | | 84 | 29 |
| Congo | Petroleum | — | 62 | France | 26 | 22 |
| | Wood | 61 | 19 | FRG | 31 | — |
| | | | | Italy | — | 15 |
| | Total | 61 | 79‡ | | 57 | 37 |
| Equatorial | | | | | | |
| Guinea | n.a. | | | n.a. | | |
| Gabon | Petroleum | 16 | 81 | France | 56 | 20 |
| | Wood | 49 | .— | FRG | 16 | — |
| | Uranium | 11 | — | U.S. | — | 18 |
| | Total | 76 | 81 | | 72 | 38 |
| Rwanda | Coffee | 12 | 63 | U.S. | | 40 |
| | Tin | 79 | 13 | U.K. | | 21 |
| | | | | Belgium | | 17 |
| | Total | 91† | 76 | | | 78 |
| Zaire | Copper | 64 | 63 | Belgium | 47 | 39 |
| | Coffee | 10 | 4 | U.S. | 13 | — |
| | Palm oil | 22 | — | Italy | 7 | 14 |
| | Total | 96† | 67‡ | | 67 | 53 |

### TABLE 3 (Continued)
### Composition and Direction of Exports, 1961 and 1975

| Country | Product | Composition of Trade 1961 (%) | 1975 (%) | Partner | Direction of Trade 1961 (%) | 1975 (%) |
|---------|---------|------|------|---------|------|------|
| *East Africa* | | | | | | |
| *Botswana* | Meat and produce | | 33 | | | |
| | Diamonds | | 29 | | | |
| | Copper-nickel matte | | 20 | | | |
| | Total | | 82 | | | |
| *Ethiopia* | Coffee | 50 | 31 | U.S. | 40 | 17 |
| | Oilseeds | 8 | 17 | Italy | 10 | 0 |
| | Pulses | 10 | 13 | FRG | — | 11 |
| | Total | 68 | 61 | | 50 | 28 |
| *Kenya* | Coffee | 25 | 20 | U.K. | 22 | 10 |
| | Tea | 15 | 13 | FRG | 14 | — |
| | | | | Uganda | — | 12 |
| | Total | 40‡ | 33 | | 36 | 22 |
| *Lesotho* | Wool | | 35 | South Africa | Over 50% | |
| | Mohair | | 16 | | | |
| | Live animals | | 16 | | | |
| | Total | | 67‡ | | | |
| *Madagascar* | Coffee | 29 | 27 | France | 54 | 25 |
| | Vanilla | 10 | 8 | U.S. | 15 | 15 |
| | Cloves | — | 7 | India | — | 13 |
| | Total | 39 | 42‡ | | 69 | 53 |
| *Malawi* | Tobacco | 34 | 48 | U.K. | | 35 |
| | Tea | 27 | 20 | U.S. | | 7 |
| | Sugar | — | 12 | Netherlands | | 6 |
| | Total | 61‡ | 80 | | | 48 |
| *Mauritius* | Sugar | 92 | 84 | U.K. | 81 | 77 |
| | Clothing | — | 6 | France | — | 6 |
| | | | | U.S. | 1 | 6 |
| | Total | 92 | 90 | | 82 | 89 |
| *Somalia* | Live animals | 27 | 65 | Italy | 56 | 10 |
| | Bananas | 48 | 14 | Saudi Arabia | — | 60 |
| | | | | Kuwait | — | 5 |
| | Total | 75 | 79 | | 56 | 75 |

157

### TABLE 3 (Continued)
### Composition and Direction of Exports, 1961 and 1975

| Country | Product | Composition of Trade 1961 (%) | Composition of Trade 1975 (%) | Partner | Direction of Trade 1961 (%) | Direction of Trade 1975 (%) |
|---|---|---|---|---|---|---|
| Swaziland | Sugar | | 54 | n.a. | | |
| | Wood pulp | | 9 | | | |
| | Iron ore | | 9 | | | |
| | Total | | 72 | | | |
| Tanzania | Coffee beans | 13 | 19 | U.K. | 35 | 12 |
| | Sisal | 28 | 12 | FRG | 8 | 8 |
| | Cotton | 13 | 12 | Singapore | — | 8 |
| | Total | 54 | 43 | | 43 | 28 |
| Uganda | Coffee | 29 | 75 | U.K. | 16 | 20 |
| | Cotton | 35 | 11 | U.S. | 14 | 20 |
| | Tea | 3 | 6 | Japan | — | 8 |
| | Total | 77 | 92 | | 30 | 48 |
| Zambia | Copper | 88 | 90 | U.K. | 32 | 15 |
| | Zinc | — | 4 | Japan | 11 | 17 |
| | | | | FRG | — | 14 |
| | Total | 88 | 94 | | 43 | 46 |

*1972.
†1963/64.
‡1974.
§Shipped from Guinea to Cameroon for processing.
¶1971.
SOURCES:   International Monetary Fund (IMF), *Direction of Trade*, Annual 1960–76, and 1970–76; UN, *International Trade Statistics* (1976); IMF. *International Financial Statistics*, 1977 Supplement, Annual Data 1952–76; *Africa South of the Sahara*, Europa Publication, Ltd., London, 1977–78.

## TABLE 4

### Manufacturing Activity and Output

| Country | Value of Manufacturing Output in Million $ U.S. | | Manufacturing as a Percentage of GDP at Current Factor Costs | |
|---|---|---|---|---|
| | 1960 | 1973 | 1960 | 1973 |
| West Africa | | | | |
| Benin | 0.1 | 26.5 | 4.3 | 7.6 |
| Gambia | 0.45 | 1.8 | 2.2 | 3.3 |
| Ghana | 118.6 | 220.7[a] | 9.8[b] | 10.3[d,b] |
| Guinea | 0.4[c] | 2.6 | 1.2[c,d] | 5.6[a,d] |
| Ivory Coast | 39.3 | 403.2 | 6.9[b] | 15.7 |
| Liberia | 9.3 | 26.6 | 3.7[e] | 5.7 |
| Mali | 11.7 | 34.8 | 4.7 | 9.3 |
| Mauritania | 2.0 | 9.0 | 2.6 | 3.7 |
| Niger | 10.5 | 62.9 | 4.3 | 12.6 |
| Nigeria | 150.6 | 873.7 | 4.8 | 6.0 |
| Senegal | 58.7 | 184.9 | 9.6 | 12.8 |
| Sierra Leone | 16.8[e] | 26.6 | 5.6 | 6.0 |
| Togo | 9.3 | 49.8 | 8.5 | 13.1 |
| Upper Volta | 12.6 | 61.7 | 5.6 | 14.9 |
| Central Africa | | | | |
| Burundi | 2.7[f] | 6.3[f] | 4.7[g,h] | 8.7 |
| Cameroon | 29.6[i] | 251.3[i] | 6.1 | 15.3 |
| Central Africa | 7.3 | 35.9 | 5.7 | 13.1 |
| Chad | 7.7 | 26.9 | 4.5 | 8.9 |
| Congo | 10.1 | 47.1 | 8.2 | 10.6 |
| Equatorial Guinea | — | — | — | — |
| Gabon | 7.3 | 40.8 | 6.1 | 7.6 |
| Rwanda | 0.8 | 12.3 | 0.7 | 4.3 |
| Zaire | 28.0 | 255.0 | 13.2 | 9.2 |

### TABLE 4 (Continued)
### Manufacturing Activity and Output

| Country | Value of Manufacturing Output in Million $ U.S. | | Manufacturing as a Percentage of GDP at Current Factor Costs | |
|---|---|---|---|---|
| | 1960 | 1973 | 1960 | 1973 |
| *East Africa* | | | | |
| Botswana | 2.7 | 14.5 | 8.1 | 8.9 |
| Ethiopia | 54.5 | 239.5 | 6.1 | 10.1 |
| Kenya | 68.6 | 298.4 | 9.4 | 14.3 |
| Lesotho | 0.4[e] | 2.0 | 0.9[h] | 2.8 |
| Madagascar | 22.3 | 156.9 | 4.1[b] | 12.5[b] |
| Malawi | 10.1[i] | 73.7[i] | 5.8 | 14.8 |
| Mauritius | 15.7 | 45.8 | 13.1 | 15.7 |
| Somalia | — | — | — | — |
| Swaziland | 1.5 | 18.2 | 5.3 | 13.1 |
| Tanzania | 28.2 | 174.8 | 5.1 | 10.9 |
| Uganda | 47.8 | 131.7 | 8.8 | 8.4 |
| Zambia | 23.1 | 232.0 | 4.0 | 13.4 |

[a]1972; [b]at market prices; [c]1962; [d]at constant market prices; [e]1964; [f]includes mining, gas, and electricity; [g]at constant factor costs; [h]1965; [i]includes mining.

SOURCE: World Bank, *World Tables*, International Bank for Reconstruction and Development, Washington, D.C., 1976.

to government policy, as among trade unions in Ghana and peasants in Western Nigeria, was sometimes what first shook independence regimes, previewing their later overthrow by different petit bourgeois segments.

## CONTRADICTIONS IN COMMODITY PRODUCTION AND EXPORT

At the heart of this discontent was the fact that most postcolonial regimes could not expect to significantly raise mass living standards by maintaining their reliance on traditional primary pro-

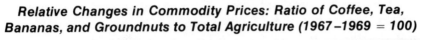

## FIGURE 1

### Relative Changes in Commodity Prices: Ratio of Coffee, Tea, Bananas, and Groundnuts to Total Agriculture (1967–1969 = 100)

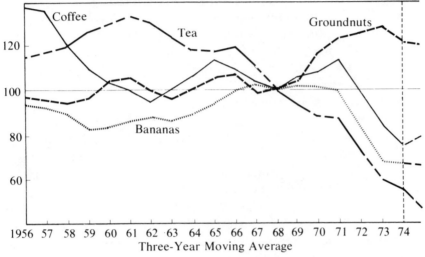

SOURCE: World Bank, *Price Forecasts for Major Primary Commodities,* p. 23.

duction exports; yet, as stressed above, this reliance had been maintained. In extreme cases such as Ghana, where the regime attempted to *increase* reliance on cocoa exports, price elasticity of demand conditions for that commodity meant that total revenues received for the crop actually fell, as prices declined markedly.[26] Prices for most primary products exported from Africa have remained very unstable, as Figure 1 illustrates for four of the major African agricultural exports. Taking the 1955–1974 period and examining the major commodity exports from black Africa, the standard deviation of prices, expressed as a percentage of the mean price for the period, reached the following levels: cocoa—21 percent, coffee—21 percent, tea—23 percent,

[26]Price elasticity of demand for cocoa has been estimated at −0.13 to −0.4; i.e., for every 10 percent increase in quantity supplied on the market, price would fall 30 percent, *ceteris paribus*. Thus total revenue would fall (and did in Ghana). See World Bank, *Price Forecasts for Major Primary Commodities,* Report 814, Commodities and Export Projections Div., Economic Analysis and Projections Dept., Washington, D.C., 1975.

groundnuts—10 percent, sisal—28 percent, cotton—10 percent, copper—26 percent, iron ore—26 percent, and manganese ore 36 percent. While the deviations for groundnuts and cotton are not that high, those for the other commodities most certainly are.[27] Such price changes made for dramatic ups and downs in economic conditions in African societies throughout the 1960–1975 period, leaving the planning of structural change very difficult and the avoidance of periodic foreign-exchange crises almost impossible.

Moreover, the purchasing power of most African commodity exports in the international economy was declining over much of the postindependence period. Overall barter terms of trade for less developed countries declined by an average of 0.3 percent annually between 1960 and 1972, and purchasing power of those exports (excluding petroleum) declined by an annual average of 1.4 percent during that time.[28] It is true that in 1973 and 1974 there was a remarkable upsurge in commodity prices that reversed this long-run trend, but since then most commodity prices have fallen again, and the terms of trade of African countries have generally been left even worse off because of their requirements for high-priced oil imports. Table 5 provides detailed evidence of how badly the relative prices of exports have declined recently for many African countries. Table 6 complements this with detailed data on export-earnings fluctuations by country, underlining the points about uncertainty made above. Both tables provide brief comparisons with representative Organization for Economic Cooperation and Development (OECD) countries to demonstrate the contrasts evident in the more difficult African experience: except for oil exporters, terms-of-trade pressures have been significantly greater on many African countries, while fluctuations have also been far wider.

For a few African countries, the emergence of new resource exports in the postindependence period provided an escape from these constraints. Petroleum discoveries and development in Nigeria and Gabon, iron ore in Mauritania, and copper in Botswana provided such escape. In other countries, possibilities for

[27]Ibid., p. 35.
[28]Ibid., p. 4.

**TABLE 5**

**Commodity Terms-of-Trade Indices for Selected African Countries**
**(1970 = 100)**

| Country | 1956 | 1961 | 1966 | 1971 | 1975 |
|---------|------|------|------|------|------|
| *Oil exporters* | | | | | |
| Angola | 147 | 102 | 100 | 96 | 121 |
| Nigeria | 154 | 118 | 106 | 110 | 298 |
| *Most seriously affected* | | | | | |
| Ethiopia | 114 | 82 | 92 | 91 | 81 |
| Lesotho | 112 | 110 | 115 | 88 | 85 |
| Mali | 105 | 93 | 102 | 91 | 56 |
| Rwanda | 120 | 85 | 95 | 86 | 65 |
| Somalia | 103 | 88 | 96 | 96 | 79 |
| Uganda | 125 | 96 | 94 | 97 | 79 |
| Upper Volta | 98 | 88 | 93 | 101 | 70 |
| Zaire | 63 | 64 | 113 | 77 | 47 |
| Zambia | 53 | 59 | 117 | 74 | 45 |
| *OECD comparisons* | | | | | |
| Canada | 101 | 98 | 98 | 98 | 108 |
| Germany | 80 | 93 | 95 | 104 | 102 |
| U.S. | 89 | 98 | 100 | 98 | 82 |

SOURCE: A. R. M. Ritter, "Conflict and Coincidence of Canadian and Less Developed Country Interests in International Trade in Primary Commodities," Report prepared by the Economic Council of Canada, 1977, pp. 44–51.

diversification into new agricultural commodities (into cashews, for instance, in Tanzania) also existed, and in a country like Kenya, where peasant production had historically been suppressed to help settler agriculture, expanded peasant cash cropping could still provide new impetus to the economy (with new production of tea and pyrethrum especially notable). But by and large, primary product production could not provide the rapid income advances that intermediary bourgeoisies needed to finance both their own embourgeoisement *and* some significant increase in mass living standards. Political instability was the result.

These contradictions within a commodity-based strategy led regimes to try to generate economic growth and surplus accumulation through other means. In particular, postindependence

## TABLE 6

### Indices of Export Fluctuation for Selected African Countries

| Country | 1960–1965 | 1965–1970 | 1970–1975 |
|---|---|---|---|
| *Per capita income over $1,000 per year* | | | |
| Gabon | 3.3 | 6.7 | 21.7 |
| *Per capita income between $401 and $1,000 per year* | | | |
| Zambia | 9.1 | 8.2 | 20.4 |
| Ivory Coast | 6.6 | 3.9 | 13.1 |
| Congo | 12.2 | 11.2 | 10.7 |
| *Per capita income between $201 and $400 per year* | | | |
| Nigeria | 6.7 | 14.8 | 21.7 |
| Senegal | 5.7 | 6.5 | 15.0 |
| Cameroon | 6.0 | 3.8 | 14.6 |
| Ghana | 1.8 | 10.5 | 13.2 |
| Liberia | 17.1 | 1.8 | 5.9 |
| *Per capita income below $200 per year* | | | |
| Togo | 11.1 | 6.4 | 28.1 |
| Lesotho | 4.5 | 6.6 | 21.2 |
| Gambia | 9.9 | 13.6 | 17.6 |
| Zaire | 8.2 | 7.0 | 15.4 |
| Upper Volta | 19.1 | 8.1 | 12.4 |
| Guinea | 11.1 | 3.6 | 10.9 |
| Niger | 6.5 | 12.5 | 10.1 |
| Ethiopia | 3.2 | 5.4 | 8.6 |
| Somalia | 7.3 | 3.0 | 7.6 |
| Tanzania | 7.9 | 5.2 | 7.2 |
| Mali | 15.3 | 27.5 | 6.5 |
| Sierra Leone | 10.2 | 8.2 | 5.6 |
| Uganda | 7.2 | 4.8 | 3.5 |

### TABLE 6 (Continued)
### Indices of Export Fluctuation for Selected African Countries

| Country | 1960–1965 | 1965–1970 | 1970–1975 |
|---|---|---|---|
| *OECD comparisons* | | | |
| Germany | 1.2 | 2.0 | 7.8 |
| U.S. | 2.6 | 1.9 | 7.8 |
| Sweden | 1.7 | 3.5 | 5.9 |
| Japan | 4.9 | 3.6 | 5.6 |
| Canada | 3.5 | 1.6 | 5.4 |
| U.K. | 1.3 | 3.7 | 3.1 |

NOTE: These indices are annual average percentage deviations from trend of export earnings.

SOURCE: A. R. M. Ritter, op. cit. in Table 5, pp. 56–58.

economic policy in most African countries has aimed to promote import-substituting industrialization, and in many countries this effort has been paralleled by endeavors to establish regionally integrated units larger than the individual states. Yet the dynamics of these efforts have been contradictory too. They have not generated development in Africa. The two detailed sections below explore why such strategies have failed.

## IMPORT SUBSTITUTION AND TECHNOLOGY TRANSFER

Under their postindependence regimes, many African countries attempted to encourage industrialization, mainly to satisfy consumer needs that had been met formerly through imports. Though a certain amount of industrialization did result from these attempts, the character of that new manufacturing did not make a very satisfactory contribution to African development. Some of these shortcomings can be summarized as follows:

1. The expansion of manufacturing output did not bring with it an equivalent expansion of employment in the manufacturing

165

sector. Commonly, quite marked percentage increases in output during the 1955–1970 period were paralleled by low or negative changes in employment.[29]

2. Moreover, the relatively high wages often offered in the new manufacturing industries provided an important encouragement to rural-to-urban migration, leading to significant increases in open urban unemployment to rates of 10 to 15 percent in a number of African countries.[30]

3. In addition, the very high rates of import protection often established in order to encourage new industries commonly led to manufacturing prices being well above the world-price level. This situation involved the imposition of extra costs on all consumers of the products within the country and usually turned urban-rural terms of trade against the peasantry (thereby also discouraging agricultural production).

4. Such levels of protection, and resulting high-priced production, also made it very difficult for the new industries to export much of their output. Yet the new industries commonly required a good many continuing imports from abroad, of machinery and raw materials or intermediate inputs. The combination of these two considerations contributed to recurring foreign-exchange problems within African economies, especially in the face of some of the primary product revenue fluctuations noted in the previous section.

5. The small markets in most African countries, moreover, reinforced this vicious circle. They made it impossible in many cases to achieve sufficient economies of scale through internal sales to permit lowering of import-protection barriers once firms were well established; in short, high costs seemed destined to characterize the new industries over the longer run too.

6. It is also important to note that the infrastructure requirements

[29]Charles R. Frank, "Urban Unemployment and Economic Growth in Africa," *Oxford Economic Papers*, vol. 20, no. 2, 1968.

[30]David Turnham, *The Employment Problem in Less-Developed Countries*, OECD, Paris, 1971.

of the new industries seemed to push them into locating in larger urban areas, particularly the national capitals of most countries. This industrialization tended to exacerbate center-periphery gaps in income and opportunity within Africa.

The most common explanations offered for this set of effects in the recent literature rely on an analysis of interaction among inherited patterns of income distribution, trade union pressures for higher wages, and policy errors on the part of governments. Skewed income distribution, the argument suggests, meant that potential markets within Africa were mainly for those consumer goods imported to serve the demand of relatively well-off people. Import substitution of such goods became import reproduction, since the same minority market was being served by the new industries. Moreover, such reproduction required the use of capital-intensive technology similar to that used to produce such items abroad and reliance on a good many imported inputs. Thus the new manufacturing enterprises could not be expected to generate much employment or many linkages. It is often suggested as well that this set of considerations explains why foreign capital played such a major role in the new manufacturing sectors: foreign firms had obvious advantages in reproducing the goods that they already manufactured abroad. Within this perspective, some analysts went on to stress the role of trade union pressure on manufacturing wages as another major factor encouraging capital-intensive techniques and limited employment effects. At the same time, the protection policies chosen were seen as no more than mistakes by government that could be corrected.

An alternative explanation of these industrialization shortcomings deserves investigation—not so much because the more common explanation above is wholly wrong in its argument, but because the point from which that analysis starts is naive. Our explanation starts, instead, from the nature of the postindependence regimes, as described above, and from the change in metropolitan economic strategy toward periphery African countries, identified in the earlier discussion of independence. That change involved a shift from reliance on metropolitan trading houses to emphasis on direct investment to accumulate capital in periphery countries.

The industrialization undertaken in postindependence Africa was therefore usually within the context of multinational enterprise and was shaped by that context. Thus 43 percent of the paid-up capital in manufacturing in Ethiopia was foreign-owned in 1969–1970 and an even larger share was foreign-controlled.[31] Similarly, at least 43 percent of the 1971 manufacturing output in Kenya was produced by subsidiaries;[32] 71 percent of the capital of Cameroonian manufacturing firms in 1974–1975 was foreign-owned;[33] 58 percent of the paid-up capital in Nigerian manufacturing activities in 1971 was foreign-owned;[34] and 85 percent of the "modern" manufacturing sector in Senegal was foreign-owned in the early 1970s.[35]

The character of the industrialization that took place, then, reflected the international strategy of multinational manufacturing firms. Such a strategy, in an international business environment in which returns on product innovation and differentiation were at the heart of corporate profitability, inevitably emphasized subsidiary production of the particular trademarked products on which multinationals had built the rest of their world market. Such specific products would lend themselves to the collection of monopoly rents through the subsidiary.

This is the pattern that has emerged in Africa. Investigation of most multinational manufacturing investment in Kenya showed that the great majority of subsidiaries (69 percent) produced in Kenya only those products their parent companies had been producing in the developed countries. This product choice, in

[31]UNCTAD, *Major Issues Arising from the Transfer of Technology—A Case Study of Ethiopia*, TD/B/AC.11/21, June 1974.

[32]Steven W. Langdon, "Multinational Corporations in the Political Economy of Kenya," Ph.D. thesis, Sussex University, Sussex, England, 1976, pp. 82–92.

[33]*Afrique Industrie*, no. 127, November 15, 1976, p. 94.

[34]M. Berger, *Industrialisation Policies in Nigeria*, Afrika Studien, no. 88, Institut für Wirtschaftsforschung, Munich, 1975, pp. 161–163.

[35]Rita Cruise O'Brien, "Factors of Dependence: Senegal and Kenya," Anglo-French Colloquium on Independence and Dependence, Paris, 1976, p. 15.

turn, was statistically related to more capital-intensive choices of technology, to lower reliance on local production inputs, to *significantly higher profitability*,[36] and to lower export sales. Let us explore these employment, linkage, entrepreneurial, and income effects in more detail.

The particular kinds of products transferred for manufacturing by multinationals—with high-quality characteristics and considerable standardization requirements—often preclude adoption of less sophisticated labor-intensive production technology.[37] It is through the choice of product made by the parent corporation of an African subsidiary that the negative impact on employment noted above is produced.

Research on the construction sector in East Africa has illustrated this product-choice impact on employment. In Kenya, for instance, there are wide differences in production technology between synthetic and cotton textile manufacturing. For a similar value of output, cotton textile firms used some 50 percent more employees and less than half the capital employed by the synthetic textile subsidiary in Kenya. Clearly subsidiary promotion of synthetics as a substitute for cotton in clothing leads to lower employment effects. The same point can be made about the promotion of brand-name detergents as a substitute for laundry soap in Africa and represents an impact that could be generalized across a wide range of sectors. In such sectors, multinational

[36]"Kenyan evidence from 29 reporting manufacturing subsidiaries in 1972 showed after tax profits plus fees to total 22.8% of subsidiary capital employed, compared to parent company equivalents of 8.8%." Langdon, "Technology Transfer by Multinational Corporations in Africa: Effects on the Economy," *Africa Development*, vol. 2, no. 2, 1977, p. 99.

[37]For a general discussion, see Frances Stewart, *Technology and Under-Development*, Macmillan, England, 1977; for the Kenyan case, see Stewart, "Manufacture of Cement Blocks in Kenya," in A. S. Bhalla (ed.), *Technology and Employment in Industry*, OECD Development Centre, Paris, 1975, pp. 85–121, and Langdon, "Multinational Corporations in Kenya," p. 201; for Nigeria, see L. Schatzel, *Industrialization in Nigeria: A Spatial Analysis*, Afrika Studien, no. 81, Humanities Press, New Jersey, 1974, p. 45; and for Senegal, see World Bank, *Senegal: Tradition, Diversification and Economic Development*, International Bank for Reconstruction and Development (IBRD), Washington, D.C., 1974, p. 154.

corporations (MNCs) promote sophisticated, standardized substitutes for the satisfaction of basic human needs—from Coca-Cola for the satisfaction of thirst to Mercedes cars for the satisfaction of transport needs.

In order for domestic enterprises to compete locally with multinational subsidiaries, the former are pushed into the production of similar more sophisticated, trademarked, standardized products. This movement generates a need to license these more capital-intensive production processes and brings about significant new costs for the use of this imported technology. It results, moreover, in a reduction in the employment effects of these domestic firms.

This dynamic is apparent in many African countries. In Nigeria, for example, MNC investment has also concentrated in capital-intensive product sectors and has produced few employment benefits. In Senegal, where MNC investments constitute the bulk of the investments in manufacturing, the substantial increase in manufacturing output in the 1960s was marked by a lack of growth in employment as capital intensity was increased by these firms.

What can we conclude about MNC linkage effects? The inducement effects of an investment on further investments have been traditionally stressed in development theory, particularly with respect to industrialization. MNC investments with their emphasis on standardized products, however, severely impede the development of local linkages, since product differentiation cuts down the demand for material inputs that do not conform to the product specifications and/or the technological sophistication of the process. Furthermore, the financial benefits derived by MNCs from transfer pricing are enlarged to the extent that a subsidiary purchases its inputs from within the parent company's global network.[38]

[38]For a discussion of these effects for Kenya, see Langdon, "Technology Transfer by Multinational Corporations in Africa," p. 102; for Sierra Leone, see Killick, "The Benefits of Foreign Direct Investment and Its Alternatives: An Empirical Exploration," *Journal of Development Studies*, vol. 9, no. 2, 1973; for Nigeria, see E. C. Edozien, "Linkages, Direct Foreign Investment

An analysis of Kenyan subsidiaries reveals that they indeed import virtually all of their machinery and that most of them import over 70 percent of their material inputs. Similarly, a comparison of subsidiary and domestic methods of diamond mining in Sierra Leone underlines the subsidiary's very low linkages. In Nigeria and Senegal the linkage effects of foreign enterprise have been small. Finally, case studies of Tanzanian MNC projects have also called attention to the heavy import intensity of such manufacturing production. Generally, then, the standardized and/or differentiated characteristics of MNC products transferred, the related capital intensity of MNC production technology, and the integrated-exchange emphasis within MNC firms have all combined to create social costs rather than social benefits, in comparison with potential alternatives.

One can carry this further by looking at the MNC impact on indigenous entrepreneurship and learning. The benefits derived by the host country from direct investment by MNCs result from the spillover that occurs through positive externalities from which the MNC cannot reap profits. MNCs, therefore, might make a negative contribution because their technologies, which are more capital-intensive than those required in the host country, are imitated by local entrepreneurs. The training of local labor is a positive contribution only if these workers go on to work for national firms. It can be negative when local managers leave the host country to work abroad, thus accelerating the "brain drain."[39]

Although the data are not as rich here as in our examination of employment and linkage effects, what is available once again

---

and Nigeria's Economic Development," *Nigerian Journal of Economic Social Studies*, July 1968; for Senegal, see United States government, *Area Handbook for Senegal*, 1974, p. 305; and for Tanzania, see Andrew C. Coulson, "Tanzania's Fertilizer Factory," *Journal of Modern African Studies*, vol. 15, no. 1, March 1977, pp. 119–125.

[39]For a theoretical discussion, see Richard Caves, "Multinational Firms, Competition and Productivity in Host Country Industries," *Economica*, vol. 41, May 1974; and Ernest Tironi, "Customs Union Theory in the Presence of Foreign Firms," paper read to the Conference on a New International Economic Order, Madison, Wisc., November 11 and 12, 1977; for Kenya, see Langdon,

adds up to a largely negative balance sheet. Evidence from Kenya reveals that MNC subsidiaries have made very few efforts to develop any local African subcontractors. Officials of Kenya's indigenous industrial estates program have tried to persuade MNC subsidiaries to work with them to develop local input sources from the estates but have encountered considerable resistance. The logic of a subsidiary's integration into a global network with well-established and efficient supply channels thus collided with the developmental logic of spurring local entrepreneurship through subcontracting. Not only has MNC investment not encouraged the development of local manufacturing activities, but data from the shoe and soap industries in Kenya reveal that MNC production has undercut small-scale African producers. It has forced many domestic entrepreneurs with the skill, for example, to manufacture shoes to limit their activity to shoe repairs or, in the case of soap manufacture, obliged these firms to shift from the manufacture of simpler cleaning aids to MNC-type production or consumption technology. Signs of similar effects elsewhere in Africa imply that Kenya is not atypical. The same conclusion has been drawn on the basis of Tanzanian experience, it is reflected in complaints among Senegalese businessmen about foreign domination, and it is evident in Nigeria in the inequalities of MNC-indigenous competition there.

As to learning effects, study of the Andean Pact, while not yet duplicated for the African region, shows a more subtle effect of MNC investment. The reliance of local firms on foreign tech-

---

"Technology Transfer in Africa," and K. A. Ng'eng, "Industrial Estates as an Instrument of Economic Development," *East African Management Journal*, vol. 6, no. 4, September 1972; for Tanzania, see Brian Van Arkadie, "Private Foreign Investment: Some Limitations," in Philip A. Thomas (ed.), *Private Enterprise and the East African Company*, Kelley Publishers, Fairfield, N.J., 1969; for Senegal, see J. D. DeWilde, *The Development of African Private Enterprise*, vol. 2, IBRD, Washington, D.C., 1971, p. 1; for Nigeria, see O. Teriba, E. C. Edozien, and M. O. Kayode, "Some Aspects of Ownership and Control Structure of Business Enterprise in a Developing Economy: The Nigerian Case," *Nigerian Journal of Economic and Social Studies*, vol. 14, no. 1, 1972; and for the Andean Pact, see Lynn K. Mytelka, "Technology Dependence in the Andean Group," *International Organization*, vol. 32, no. 1, Winter 1978, pp. 101–140.

nology licensing, which such entrepreneurs feel is essential to meet multinational consumption and production technology transfer competition, breeds a technological dependence among local firms which makes them less able in the future to develop new products on their own. Import reproduction rather than import substitution is likely to continue and with it the preponderant benefits reaped by the multinational corporation.

Finally, a few words should be said about income and balance-of-payments effects, as it is in this context that the strongest conventional case has been made for direct foreign investment. Essentially it is argued that direct foreign investment contributes missing factors of production—capital and technology—thereby permitting the more productive use of existing factors. These contributions in turn generate faster expansions in national income than would otherwise take place. If, for structural reasons [such as the absence of a capital-goods sector in a less developed country (LDC) in which industrialization is accelerating], foreign-exchange constraints represent a separate and additional block on income growth, then the foreign-exchange inflows associated with foreign direct investment can have even greater income effects.

Recent studies question this conventional view. Social cost-benefit analyses of various investment projects in Kenya and India have shown positive net present values in some cases, but in certain import-substitution cases there are *negative* net present values. This outcome reflects high tariff barriers that have been effected in establishing these projects. UNCTAD studies have made this variability in impact on net income and balance of payments even more obvious. Of some 88 sample firms in India, Iran, Jamaica, and Kenya, it was found that 26 showed negative net effects, compared with the most likely alternative had the foreign investment not taken place.[40] When import-substitution projects are compared with the alternative of importing the product involved, income effects may be even more questionable.

[40]Sanjaya Lall, "Effects of Private Foreign Investment in Developing Countries: Summary of Case Studies of India, Iran, Jamaica, and Kenya," UNCTAD, TD/134/Supp. 1, April 1972.

Social-cost-benefit analyses of the import-substituting subsidiaries suggest that the majority cost LDCs a significant amount in terms of real resources and consumption.[41]

It may, of course, be argued that the trade restrictions that explain these negative effects are exogenous state policies, a view of tariff policies that fails to take account of the political economy of tariff setting as argued above. But the usual rationale for such restrictions, and for the national income costs they entail, is the positive external benefits in the form of employment, linkage, learning, and entrepreneurial effects that flow from the projects. As the above analysis has shown, the extent of such externalities in the context of foreign direct investment is, relative to local alternatives, highly questionable.

In sum, it would appear to be the nature of multinational manufacturing enterprise that accounts for many of the shortcomings of import-substituting industrialization in Africa, rather than the factors stressed in the more common explanation: skewed income distribution, high wages, narrow markets, geographical concentration. These factors were used to justify the maintenance and creation of regional common markets in post-independence Africa. Indeed, evidence on wage and salary levels paid by multinational subsidiaries suggests that they are contributing significantly to wider disparities in income distribution rather than just responding in their product choice to the disparities that already exist.

Nor does the pattern of import protection emerge as a simple government policy mistake from this perspective. Rather, import protection is seen to be the major demand for which multina-

[41]Grant L. Reuber et al., *Private Foreign Investment for Development*, Oxford University Press, New York, 1973, p. 180. Skepticism about the income effects of the foreign enterprise is strengthened by case studies of industries where the technological superiority of such enterprise is especially clear, as in Killick's study of diamond mining in Sierra Leone. See Killick, "The Benefits of Direct Foreign Investment." Killick compares an indigenous bucket-and-shovel scheme for diamond extraction with the highly mechanized foreign subsidiaries that dominated the industry and finds that high subsidiary outflows for capital equipment, dividends, and material imports mean that the indigenous scheme returns much more to the local economy from each unit of output extracted.

tionals have bargained with African governments. This import protection has usually given larger multinational subsidiaries very considerable market dominance within African countries, secure from foreign import competition. The African state has even been important, on occasion, in giving multinational subsidiaries important advantages in competition with locally controlled firms. Thus the common convention on investment in the Customs and Economic Union of Central Africa (Union Douaniere et Economique de l'Afrique Centrale, UDEAC)[42] provides for the full repatriation of capital and profits for multinational corporations even in the event exchange controls are imposed. MNCs also receive duty-free imports of capital and intermediate goods, five-year exemptions on corporate income tax, fiscal stabilization agreements, and temporary exoneration from other domestic taxes. None of these provisions is automatically granted to nationally owned firms.[43]

The willingness of African governments to provide such assistance to the multinationals can be understood in terms of the postindependence social dynamics discussed above. The petit bourgeois forces that control the institutions of the state were anxious to improve their intermediary position in the economy and could be expected, therefore, to conflict with the interests of metropolitan trading companies. But such was not necessarily the case with direct-investment projects. In fact, opportunities for embourgeoisement expanded as African traders were made the agents for subsidiary sales. The state could and did bargain out a relationship with multinationals that involved, on the one

[42]On December 8, 1964, the Presidents of Chad, the Central African Empire, the Congo–Brazzaville, Gabon, and Cameroon signed the UDEAC treaty that went into force in December 1965. Three years later Chad withdrew, and a four-member UDEAC has continued since January 1969.

[43]S. R. Dixon-Fyle, "Economic Inducements to Private Foreign Investment in Africa," *Journal of Development Studies*, vol. 4, no. 1, 1967; Langdon, "Multinational Corporations in Kenya"; H. Kristensen, "The Technology Problem in Rural Small-Scale Industries—A Case Study from Kenya," Working Paper 7, OECD Study Group on Low-Cost Technology and Rural Industrialization, Paris, September 1974; and G. Ngango, *Les Investissements d'Origine extérieure en Afrique francophone*, Presence Africaine, Paris, 1973.

side, protection for new subsidiaries (as above) and, on the other, a guaranteed role for representatives of the African petit bourgeoisie in the new manufacturing industry structure—as subsidiary executives, minority shareholders, commercial agents, directors, etc. The difficulties that the emerging African bourgeoisie was experiencing in accumulating capital were thus eased by organizing a share for them in the accumulation of the subsidiaries. The high profitability of the import-reproducing subsidiaries, with their market power, meant that they could generate such surplus readily for appropriation. In a sense, a symbiosis— or commonality of interest—thus emerged between the multinationals and the African state (and the emerging bourgeoisie that relied on that state).

This symbiosis could operate to attenuate conflicts with other politically relevant segments of the society as well. The willingness of multinational subsidiaries, for instance, to pay higher than prevailing wages permitted the neutralization of important potential trade union opponents to the existing system. And the skewing of income distribution that the postindependence regimes defended and extended *did* provide the ongoing market for many of the developed-country products the multinationals were transferring.

Where such multinational manufacturing investment continued to expand and where state institutions could operate to smooth out some of the inherent conflicts between local and foreign capital in such a context, African regimes could achieve longevity and fairly respectable growth rates (as in Kenya and the Ivory Coast). But the contradictions of such industrialization still emerged—in the unemployment, widened income disparity, internal locational imbalances, lack of linkages, and poor export performances noted above. A marked MNC role, though, permitted these regimes to face these contradictions with greater political strength, and this large MNC stake in such economies undoubtedly encouraged other metropolitan efforts to maintain such regimes through aid and military assistance.

In many instances, however, continued expansion of multinational investment was simply not feasible in the very limited markets that faced subsidiaries in many African countries. In such conditions, both local African bourgeoisies and international capital were forced to consider other strategies that would escape, at least temporarily, some of the negative constraints of the import-substitution process that had been taking place. A particularly important strategy in this respect was market expansion through regional integration.

## THE CONTRADICTIONS OF REGIONAL INTEGRATION STRATEGIES

Prior to independence, regional integration systems responded to the economic needs of the imperial powers rather than to the development concerns of the African people. In order to minimize their financial commitments, coordinate markets, establish common currency areas under their control, and create those transportation networks required to link periphery areas to coastal centers, France and Britain promoted the formation of federations, common service organizations, and common banking systems among their colonies. In this they were encouraged by business interests in the metropole, their subsidiaries in Africa, and local expatriate business communities.

In the postindependence period, international capital favored the formation of free trade areas from which it stood to benefit. But it also sought to undermine those regional integrative systems that through planning might inhibit its freedom of action. MNCs are particularly reluctant to promote regional integration if they already have a medium- or large-size market and some limited local industrial capacity. Two explanations are offered for this behavior. First, MNCs seek to maximize long-run surplus not only by minimizing costs but also by maximizing the difference between costs and sales. As a result market segmentation can create production inefficiencies that are more than compensated for by increases in sales. Second, MNCs seek to avoid risks, from competition, for example, and gain acceptable or growing market shares. Where a given MNC has located parallel activities in several of the integrating countries and where each of these subsidiaries is integrated vertically within the parent corporate structure, there is a clear disincentive to further horizontal integration and specialization with all the risks this might entail if the integrative system fragmented. New entrants may have a slightly more flexible attitude than existing firms, but even they would oppose industrial planning schemes that by rationalizing production might reduce the number of enterprises and exclude them from the market or might result in lower external tariff protection.[44] As the MNCs play a large role in African political economies, understanding their role in integration efforts is of particular importance.

Most Third World integrative systems are characterized by substantial economic disparities among the member states. To compensate less industrially developed partners for the unequal distribution of the gains that generally resulted from the liberalization of trade, a variety of fiscal and planning mechanisms were incorporated in integrative treaties. The failure to implement regional industrial planning schemes and the ineffectiveness of other compensatory mechanisms heightened conflicts over cost-benefit issues within these integrative systems. In some integrative systems (the Organisation pour la mise en valeur de la Vallée du Fleuve Sénégal, for example), these conflicts led to the transformation of the association and its abandonment of planning objectives. In others (such as the Economic Community of West Africa, ECOWAS) cost-benefit conflicts led to numerous postponements in the signing of the treaty and subsequently delays in the application of key harmonization provisions contained in this treaty. In still others (the East African Community, for example), conflicts over cost-benefit issues led to persistent crises and ultimately to a situation tantamount to dissolution.

The contemporary crisis of regional integration in Africa is not, however, a purely nationalistic affair in which states are pitted against each other in conflicts over the interstate distribution of the gains from integration. Rather, this interstate conflict is a reflection of more fundamental problems that are associated with the distribution of gains between national and

---

[44]Constantine Vaitsos, "Crisis in Regional Economic Cooperation (Integration) Among Developing Countries," *World Development*, forthcoming.

international capital as the MNC seeks to structure not only national but also regional markets around its own needs and interests.

An analysis of the Customs and Economic Union of Central Africa permits an exploration of these problems. In particular it provides an excellent case study of the way in which MNCs derive benefits from regional integration, first by maintaining market segmentation, in this instance through the operation of the "single-tax" system, and then by thwarting regional planning efforts designed to rationalize production and compensate UDEAC's less industrialized member states, Chad and the Central African Empire.

The single-tax system was set up in accordance with Articles 59 and 60 of the UDEAC Treaty. It provided that goods *manufactured* within UDEAC and sold in more than one of its member states would be subject to a tax imposed at the factory. This tax, with rates fixed collectively by the UDEAC ministerial management committee, is levied to the exclusion of all import duties or taxes on goods used in the manufacturing process and of domestic taxation on the finished product. The rate of the single tax is always lower than the customs duty that would otherwise have applied to these manufactured goods. This is in keeping with the original conception of the single tax as a mechanism designed (1) to enhance the competitive position of "local" manufactures relative to foreign imports by reducing the overall rates of taxation when compared with the common external tariff and (2) to provide each of the member states with the possibility of recovering a certain percentage of the revenues it otherwise would have earned through tariffs imposed on third-party imports. All manufactured goods to be traded within UDEAC must be accorded a single tax rate, and the proceeds from this tax are reapportioned to the member states in accordance with their consumption of these imports.

During the negotiations that led to the creation of UDEAC, delegates from Chad and the Central African Empire argued that uniform rates of taxation would unfairly advantage the more industrialized countries, whose industries were older, larger, and more efficient. As compensation for these unequal trade advantages, they proposed a variable "single" tax rate. This principle was accepted. Under the system of variable rates, plastic sandals manufactured by the Bata subsidiary in Cameroon were thus assessed in 1969–1970 at a rate of 33 percent when sold in the Central African Empire (CAE) as against the rate of 13 percent that would apply to the same item (item 64.01.11—see Table 7) when manufactured by the Bata subsidiary in the CAE. By permitting the single tax to vary, UDEAC decision makers encouraged continued segmentation of the regional market, as multinational firms that dominated the industrial sectors in the UDEAC countries now had no incentive to rationalize production. To the contrary, market segmentation fit nicely into the profit-maximization strategy of the multinational firm under existing high-cost-production conditions.

By focusing solely on the state level in their debates over the costs and benefits of integration, UDEAC leaders failed to realize the extent to which this system benefited the MNC above all. The clearest such benefits are from trade. As most single-tax firms are foreign-owned, international capital became the net beneficiary of the intraregional trade in manufactures. Although data on ownership structure are incomplete, where data were available it was found that, in 1969, fully 68 percent of the Cameroonian single-tax firms (39 of 57) were foreign-owned and only two were owned by Cameroonian nationals. Data for the re-

**TABLE 7**

*Rates of the Single Tax for Item 64.01.11 in 1969–1970 (%)*

| Producer | Consumer | | | | |
| --- | --- | --- | --- | --- | --- |
| | *Cameroon* | *CAE* | *Congo* | *Gabon* | *Chad* |
| *Bata (Cameroon)* | 25 | 33 | 33 | 32 | 33 |
| *Bata (CAE)* | 18 | 13 | 18 | 15 | * |
| *Bata (Congo)* | 18 | 18 | 18 | 16 | 18 |

*Chad withdrew from UDEAC before the Bata subsidiary in the CAE had received single tax rates for its products.

SOURCE:  Union Douaniere et Economique de l'Afrique Centrale, *Journal Oficiel de l'UDEAC*, diverse issues 1966–1970.

maining firms were not accessible. Similarly, 53 percent of the CAE single-tax firms (11 of 21), 55 percent of the Congolese firms (12 of 22), 80 percent of the Gabonese firms (4 of 5), and 36 percent of the Chadian firms (4 of 11) for which ownership data could be found were foreign-owned.[45]

To appreciate the extent to which the single-tax system facilitated the restructuring of markets and reinforced the market dominance of multinational firms, this mechanism must be taken in conjunction with the UDEAC investment code. Together these mechanisms operated to favor the multinational firm over national competitors by granting numerous fiscal, tariff, and infrastructural incentives to foreign firms willing to locate in the UDEAC region. By cheapening capital through these incentives, the single-tax system and investment code encouraged the overbuilding of plant capacity. At the same time, the small size of individual UDEAC markets implied that these overbuilt factories would operate below capacity and at high cost, thus diverting resources into inefficient productive activities. The single-tax system and investment code, moreover, guaranteed the oligopolistic market conditions that permitted the multinational firm to pass along its higher costs to the consumer, all the while maintaining high profits. By inducing the MNCs to import intermediate and capital goods through the provision of tax and tariff benefits on such imports, the single-tax system and investment code reduced the likelihood that MNCs would establish backward or forward linkages within the domestic or regional economy and increased the incentive to transfer trademarked products and capital-intensive processes to the region. The single-tax system thus induced MNCs to enter the UDEAC market and remain within it despite mounting evidence that they duplicated existing capacity, produced inefficiently, transferred inappropriate product and process technologies, and drained surplus from UDEAC economies through substantial duty-free imports and profit repatriation. The shoe industry illustrates these

[45]David Kom, *Le Cameroun Essai d'Analyse économique et politique*, Editions Sociales, Paris, 1971; and G. Ngango, *Les Investissements d'Origine Extérieure en Afrique francophone*, pp. 305–316.

arguments, but they could as easily be substantiated with data for beverages, tobacco, textiles, food, clothing, or other consumer goods that dominate in single-tax production and trade.

By 1966 six shoe factories—two in Cameroon, two in the Central African Empire, and two in the Congo and all of them foreign-owned—had located in the UDEAC region. Combined annual capacity was over 7 million pairs of shoes, but production in 1966 totaled only 3.6 million pairs of shoes, or about 50 percent of capacity.[46] Three of these firms produced both plastic sandals and leather or canvas shoes, one firm manufactured only leather shoes, and two of the firms manufactured only plastic sandals. Five of the six firms, therefore, produced a product—plastic sandals—for which all molding and extruding equipment and all the intermediate inputs of polyvinylchloride (PVC) had to be imported. Moreover, only the Cameroonian plants could use domestic sources of leather in shoe manufacture, although it might be argued that Congolese and Centrafrican imports of leather from Chad and Cameroon constituted backward linkages within the regional context. Yet it is precisely the production of plastic sandals that is being promoted by foreign-owned firms. In 1967 production and consumption of leather and canvas shoes in Cameroon, the CAE, the Congo, and Gabon was valued at 239,112,000 F CFA[47] as opposed to a production and consumption of plastic sandals totaling 180,910,000 F CFA. By 1971 production and consumption of plastic sandals in these four countries had risen to 620,156,000 F CFA, an increase of 71 percent over the 1967 figure, and production and consumption of leather and canvas shoes had fallen to 226,607,000, a decrease of 5.2 percent over this four-year period. (See Table 8.)

Despite the underutilization of capacity and the relatively slow growth of the UDEAC market for footwear, by 1972 two additional firms had begun production. In Cameroon, the SACC,

---

[46]P. Borel, *Problems of Plan Implementation: Economic Cooperation and Integration in Central Africa*, UN Doc. E/AC.54/L.26/Add. 3, New York, 1968, p. 62; and Communauté Economique Européenne, *Possibilités d'Industrialisation des États Africaines et Malagache Associés*, Series II, Brussels, 1967, pp. 11, 36, 61, 64.

[47]CFA = communauté financière africaine; for 1969–70, $1.00 ≅ 250 CFA.

### TABLE 8

### Production and Consumption of Footwear in 1967 and 1971

| Producers of Item 64.01.11, Plastic Sandals | | (1,000 F CFA) Consumers of the Product | | | | | |
|---|---|---|---|---|---|---|---|
| | | Cameroon | CAE | Congo | Gabon | Chad | Total |
| Cameroon Bata (F), Emen's Industry (F) | 1971 | 399,160 (77%) | 53,969 | 24,222 | 42,777 | — | 520,128 |
| | 1967 | 71,579 (49%) | 50,358 | 570 | 1,488 | 23,112 | 147,107 |
| CAE Bata (F), Moura & Gouveia (F) | 1971 | 4,246 | 88,855 (95%) | — | 120 | — | 93,221 |
| | 1967 | — | 49,644 (69%) | 41 | — | 22,621 | 72,306 |
| Congo Bata (F), Africa-Plast (F) | 1971 | — | — | 6,504 (96%) | 303 | — | 6,807 |
| | 1967 | — | 3,000 | 4,230 (59%) | — | — | 7,230 |
| Producers of Items 64.02.21 and 64.02.22, Canvas and Leather Shoes Cameroon Bata (F), SACC (U) | 1971 | 145,586 (75%) | 12,047 | 16,212 | 20,303 | — | 194,148 |
| | 1967 | 139,529 (73%) | 24,348 | 7.074 | 10,169 | 10,576 | 191,696 |
| CAE Bata (F), Moura & Gouveia (F), Splendor (U) | 1971 | 905 | 2,626 (72%) | — | 107 | — | 3,638 |
| | 1967 | — | 38,610 (74%) | 143 | — | 12,953 | 51,706 |

**TABLE 8 (Continued)**
**Production and Consumption of Footwear in 1967 and 1971**

| Producers of Item 64.01.11, Plastic Sandals | | (1,000 F CFA) Consumers of the Product | | | | | |
|---|---|---|---|---|---|---|---|
| | | Cameroon | CAE | Congo | Gabon | Chad | Total |
| *Congo* | | | | | | | |
| Bata (F) | 1971 | — | 1,540 | 26,400 (92%) | 881 | — | 28,821 |
| | 1967 | — | 6,654 | 11,777 (58%) | 808 | 1,084 | 20,323 |

*F = foreign-owned, U = ownership unknown, % = figures in percentages are domestic consumption as a percentage of total production of the given single-tax product.

NOTE: These tables do not deal exhaustively with all shoe and sandal products. Production in category 64.02.29, "Other Shoes," which declined dramatically from 1967 to 1971, has been excluded.

SOURCE: UDEAC, *Bulletin des Statistiques Générales de l'UDEAC*, no. 22, April 1968, and no. 38, April 1972.

whose ownership structure is unknown, was established in 1968 for the purpose of manufacturing leather shoes and by 1972 was producing some 500,000 pairs annually at full capacity. A year later, however, the Bata shoe company opened its Centrafrican subsidiary with a capacity of 1.5 million pairs of plastic, leather, and canvas shoes. By 1972 that firm's production was only 750,000 pairs, or some 50 percent of capacity.[48] In the same year the Congolese Bata subsidiary was producing at only 50 percent of capacity. Nevertheless, protected by the common external tariff from outside competition, protected by the single-tax system from competition within UDEAC, and encouraged by the Centrafrican leadership to establish in that country, through the awarding of special tariff and tax concessions, another shoe company, linked to the industrialized countries for its supply of machinery and intermediate products, came into existence.

The search by African petit bourgeoisies for strategies to foster their own embourgeoisement while providing some rise in mass

[48]*Afrique Industrie*, 1973.

standards of living inexorably led national leaders to adopt a national perspective on regional planning within UDEAC. They thus tended to evaluate gains from integration in the industrial sector on a one-to-one basis, looking competitively at the industrial progress of one's partners and demanding compensation when one's own progress appeared more limited. This tendency toward nationalistic competition within UDEAC was exacerbated by the independent and competitive search for direct foreign investment, as MNCs could and did take advantage of such competition to encourage derogations from regional planning measures. Competition among UDEAC states for direct foreign investment, moreover, would provide multinational firms with opportunities to restructure the regional market to their own needs, thereby reinforcing their oligopolistic control over national markets. The evolution of the textile industry in UDEAC provides only one example of how this restructuring has been accomplished.

With French government encouragement, the Agache-Willot group founded the first Equatorial African textile mill, Industrie Textile Centrafricaine (INTEC), at Boali in 1953 in what is now the Central African Empire. This mill was intended to serve all of French Equatorial Africa. Ten years later, with independence, the two other cotton producers in the region, Chad and Cameroon, signed a protocol envisaging the construction of two textile plants, one a spinning and weaving factory at Fort Archambault (Chad) and the other a bleaching and printing plant, using the unbleached cloth from Chad, at Garoua in northern Cameroon. In addition to vertical integration, the agreement between the two governments included a proposal to specialize production so that the entire Cameroonian market would be reserved for Chadian production of the broadcloth known as *tissue de pagnes* while the Chadian market would be supplied with other kinds of printed cloth from Cameroon. Initiative for this bilateral, intergovernmental arrangement came from a number of prominent French and German groups that took a majority of the shares in these two companies.

In 1964 the CAE government and private firms had created the Industrie Cotonnière Centrafricaine (ICCA) (Agache-Willot, 56 percent), which merged with INTEC a few years later. Without knowledge of the Chadian-Cameroonian agreement and under the assumption that its dominant place in the Chadian market was assured, ICCA developed an ambitious program for the expansion and diversification of its production of cotton textiles. It was not until the CAE sought preferential tax treatment for ICCA under the new UDEAC investment code that the conflict was brought out into the open, and then it was pitched not at the level of MNC manipulation but at interstate competition and the need for compensation. In view of the historical position of the textile industry in the CAE and what was believed to be a growing textile market in UDEAC, the management committee granted ICCA a number of tax and tariff concessions. This did not end but rather began the competitive race for new MNC entrants into the UDEAC market and for the efforts of existing firms to enlarge their market shares at the expense of the CAE firms.

Within the next few years the Cotonnière Industrielle du Cameroun—Société Textile du Tchad (CICAM-STT) agreement was revised and the specialization agreement abandoned. In 1968 the Congo accepted an offer from the People's Republic of China to build a textile plant at Kisoundi, Société Textiles du Congo (SOTEXCO)—now a state-owned corporation. In April 1969 the Gabonese created the Société Industrielle Textile du Gabon (SOTEGA), a printing and dyeing plant based on cloth imported not from the CAE, Chad, or Cameroon but from Hong Kong. Among its owners were the Gabonese state (9 percent); SON-ADIG (6 percent); the Companie Commerciale Hollando-Africaine (42.5 percent), a new entrant into the UDEAC; Texunion-CEGEPAR; COFIMER; CICAM; Agache-Willot; and the German Deutsche Gesellschaft für Wirtschaftliche Zusammenarbeit (DEG) (42.5 percent). With the proliferation of spinning, weaving, printing, and dyeing plants in UDEAC, a new agreement among the five UDEAC *countries* had clearly become a necessity.

In April 1969 a meeting was held in Yaoundé to work out a UDEAC textile agreement. Given the emergence of a symbiotic relationship between the states and the MNCs within their national borders, it was a logical extension to institutionalize this symbiosis at the regional level. In addition to the finance and development (planning) ministers who made up the UDEAC management committee, therefore, this became the first meeting of its kind in which representatives of the industries concerned participated directly. The result was an agreement that regulated the flow of textiles among the UDEAC states through the allocation of export quotas and that provided for a careful allocation of specializations among the various textile industries.

The agreement has above all benefited those French textile interests that dominate the Cameroonian textile industry—in particular Texunion, which is a major shareholder in CICAM, STT, and SOTEGA. As the data in Table 9 illustrate, it is the annual turnover of these firms that has been rising most rapidly, and both CICAM and STT are producing near to capacity. Planned expansion of production capacity in these firms has already been announced. In contrast, neither SOTEXCO nor ICCA (which was nationalized in January 1976) has been able to increase production and both are only producing at roughly 75 percent of capacity. The UDEAC market for synthetic textiles, moreover, has also been captured by Texunion in cooperation with the French chemical firm Rhone Poulenc, which recently

**TABLE 9**

**Evolution of the Textile Industry in UDEAC**

| Firm | Turnover (million F CFA) 1971 | Turnover (million F CFA) 1975 | Production Capacity (million meters) 1975 | Production (million meters) 1971 | Production (million meters) 1975 |
|------|------|------|------|------|------|
| CICAM | 2,348 | 6,200 | 30.0 | 17.9 | 29.2 |
| STT | 1,800 | 2,600 | 15.5 | 15.2 | 14.0 |
| ICCA/ICAT | 982 | 1,300* | 17.0 | 12.1 | 12.9 |
| SOTEGA | 675 | 1,667 | 8.0 | 4.3 | 6.3 |
| SOTEXCO | 600† | 600 | 3.5 | 2.3 | 2.5 |

*1974.
†1972.

SOURCE: "Les Industries Textiles dans les États de l'Afrique," *Afrique Industrie*, No. 128, December 1, 1976, pp. 40–59.

began a major expansion of overseas production. Société Camerounaise pour la Fabrication Detissus Synthetiques (SYNTECAM), the Cameroonian synthetic textile plant that is owned jointly by CICAM, Texunion, Rhone Poulenc Textile, SCOA Industries, DEG, and the Cameroonian government, began production in 1971 and is currently utilizing 88 percent of capacity. As in the case of plastic sandals, the synthetic textile industry is based on imported intermediate and capital goods.

The above analysis reveals that the principal contradiction within these African integrative systems is the one generated by the interplay of a nationalist orientation and the distortion resulting from dependence. The link between these two variables, dependence and nationalism, passes through the class structure in each of the member countries. Thus the willingness to plan and the ability to control the regional economy in the interests of autonomously generated development remain as limited as the corresponding effort at the national level, and essentially for the same reason: the close ties between the MNC sector and the section of the petit bourgeoisie in control of the state. This linkage, it was shown, reduced the effectiveness of compensatory measures, such as the single-tax system. To the extent that MNCs sought to shape the integration process to their own needs and interests, moreover, as in the harmonization of industry, transnational linkages have exacerbated the tendency toward nationalistic competition, thus thwarting efforts at integrated planning. The result has been to shift the distribution of gains in favor of international capital and reduce the positive role of integration strategies in the development process.

In order to transform integration into an instrument of autonomous development, regional policies that regulate external linkages in the interest of domestic development must be enacted. The cornerstone of such an approach would be a set of measures through which direct foreign investment and technology transfer are collectively regulated.

Only through such regulation would it be possible to begin to break down competitive nationalism and permit the regional center to harmonize policies in such a way as to rationalize production at the same time as it more equitably distributes future productive capacity. Without joint regulation of capital imports, competition to attract foreign capital will likely continue to thwart efforts at regional industrial planning. Similarly, without the regulation of technology transfer, technology imports will remain inappropriate, will engender high costs, will result in the formation of few backward or forward linkages within the regional economy, and will result in the transfer of the ability to operate foreign technologies without the capacity to assimilate and adapt these technologies. To the extent that this pattern of technology transfer persists, new industries will be linked more closely to their foreign parent or technology supplier and segmentation of the regional political economy will continue.

While regulation of direct foreign investment and technology transfer represents the cornerstone of a new integrative system, several other policies would be required to support this structure. First, in addition to the joint regulation of direct foreign investment, a common front in negotiations with foreign aid donors should be encouraged in order to reduce competition over foreign loans and grants, promote regional consultation and planning, and limit the effectiveness of individual pressures on national leaders from foreign aid donors. Second, the secretariat itself must develop the in-house capability to formulate industrial plans. In many African integrative systems, such as the Communauté Economique de l'Afrique de l'Ouest, the Conseil de l'Entente, and the UDEAC, secretariats are staffed by expatriates on loan from foreign aid agencies. The necessary planning skills thus are not acquired by local personnel. Finally, it will be necessary to change the conception of regional industrial planning from one in which isolated products are selected and allocated among the member states in a kind of grab bag approach and replace it with one in which an entire industrial sector is planned. Only by allocating to the various member states both intermediate and finished goods within this sector can the articulation of national and regional economies be increased. Intraindustry specialization and local generation of technology to serve this sector become feasible. Joint ventures among private and/or state corporations, moreover, within the framework of sectoral plans would heighten the level of commitment to regional planning efforts.

Yet in the present African context it would be foolhardy to expect such a strategy of fuller regional integration to be readily adopted. Those most affected by the crisis of regional integration of the 1970s are primarily the inland, poor, less industrialized countries whose leadership pursued import-reproduction strategies for the rewards which they were seen to have brought coastal partners in terms of embourgeoisement. The failure of African integrative schemes thus contributed to the slow rate of industrial growth in these countries and the limited improvement in mass living standards, as prices for agricultural export commodities fluctuated and drought brought output down. Many of these regimes, in consequence, suffered considerable political instability in the late 1960s and 1970s.

Neither slow growth nor political instability, however, commends' these political economies to the wealthier, more industrialized Ivory Coast, Nigeria, or Kenya as potential partners in an integration scheme. Nor do these features induce the emergent bourgeoisies in these countries to abandon the symbiosis with international capital, which has provided them so handsomely with the means for their own embourgeoisement, and to do so in the interest of promoting an equitable balance in the gains from integration. For the dominant class in the more industrialized African countries to accept a regional integration strategy that included regional regulation of direct foreign investment and technology transfer, therefore, several of the contradictions in the present system would have to be heightened in the 1980s.

First, the serious market and balance-of-payments limitations on continued import-replacement industrialization which they are beginning to experience would have to produce a negative impact on profits and hence upon the surplus appropriable by the state for the purpose of embourgeoisement. Second, policies to reduce dependence on direct foreign investment and imported technology are most likely in countries with a national bourgeoisie that is large enough to be in competition with the MNC sector and enlists the help of the government in this effort. A national

190

bourgeoisie that has achieved this critical mass is nowhere apparent in Africa as yet. Third, one would have to imagine that the alternative of export-oriented industrialization as a means of generating surplus for embourgeoisement failed to survive in the 1980s. For to the extent that limitations on further growth of import-substituting industrialization deprive the petit bourgeoisie who control the state of continued opportunities for embourgeoisement, export-oriented industrialization can still be promoted to fill this breach. Indeed many African states are actively soliciting export-oriented industries and have created additional incentives, including exemptions from restrictions that apply to import-substituting industries, to render their countries more attractive. The congruence of African interests in attracting export-oriented industries and the interests of multinational firms in internationalizing production, moreover, make the disappearance of this option unrealistic in the 1980s.

Given the absence of these three conditions essential to the adoption of policies to regulate direct foreign investment and technology transfer, it is unlikely that such policies will be adopted or effectively implemented in Africa in the next decade. Rather, the 1980s are likely to see continued efforts at initiating regional integration and cooperation schemes, followed by continued crises in these regional integrative systems. The extent to which regional integration will serve as a strategy for African development in the coming decade will remain limited.

# FOUR

# Emerging Options for Africa

The previous sections of this study have stressed, first, how precolonial and colonial economic penetration shaped underdevelopment in Africa and, second, how the industrialization and regional integration efforts of the postcolonial period have reinforced such patterns. Increasingly in the seventies, though, new strategic options have been emerging for African countries. In particular, changes in the international economy appear to be opening up a new form of economic relationship between African countries and Western Europe, especially around the terms of the Lomé Convention.

This new form of economic relationship involves, on the one hand, an increased African role in export manufacturing for European markets and, on the other hand, provisions to stabilize and improve African export earnings from primary commodity production. As the embodiment of these new relations, the Lomé Convention has been hailed as "revolutionary" and as a model of the "new international economic order." The trade provisions of the Convention have been seen as a guarantee of African economic development, and the bargaining process by which Lomé was negotiated has been seen as representing an African escape from dependence. It might therefore be argued that this new option transcends the contradictions stressed above and will resolve the developmental dilemmas of postcolonial Africa.

We are not convinced that this is the case. In this section, we review some of the inadequacies of the new relationship, as reflected in the Lomé Convention context. We then suggest the conditions that are essential to the new relationship if it is to have a positive developmental impact—and indicate why we believe those conditions are most unlikely to be established. Finally, we add a brief judgment on the significance for Africa of wider international efforts to restructure commodity markets and accelerate export manufacturing for developed-country markets.

## AFRICA, THE CHANGING INTERNATIONAL DIVISION OF LABOR, AND THE LOMÉ CONVENTION

Increasingly in the last 5 to 10 years, particular Third World countries have begun to expand rapidly their secondary manufacturing exports to the industrialized countries. This situation reflects the emergence of a new international division of labor in which manufacturing production patterns are being internationalized across developed and less developed countries.

The changing pattern in the distribution of manufacturing activity is evident in data on broad trends in world manufacturing trade, showing LDCs raising their share of such trade from 4 percent in 1962 to about 8 percent in 1973.[49] The manufacturing export gains of certain LDCs and in certain industries have been even more dramatic: five Asian and Latin American countries (Taiwan, Hong Kong, South Korea, Mexico, and Brazil), by 1972 accounted for well over half of this LDC export trade, while LDC shares of developed-country imports had risen especially in clothing (from 18 percent in 1962 to 26 percent in 1972), in leather and footwear (from 12 percent to 17 percent), in wood products (from 11 percent to 13 percent), and in miscellaneous light manufactures (from 5 percent to 8 percent). Even more notable have been the gains since 1970 in LDC shares of OECD country import markets in some specialized product areas such as telecommunications equipment, small electrical machinery,

[49]UNCTAD, *Recent Trends and Developments in Trade in Manufactures and Semi-Manufactures*, TD/B/C.2/175, May 11, 1977.

small road vehicles, and household equipment. There is some evidence that a select few African countries are joining these Asian and Latin American export leaders. See Table 10 for data on leading African exporters.

The dramatic rise in the share of foreign subsidiaries in the manufactured exports of LDCs is as remarkable as the increase in the exports themselves. In Latin America from 1957 to 1966, subsidiaries of United States firms accounted for 65 percent of the increase in exports of manufactures. In 1971 foreign firms were responsible for 15 percent of South Korea's exports of manufactures, 20 percent of Taiwan's, and 50 percent of Singapore's.[50] But these figures do not tell the whole story, for they do not reveal the magnitude of intrafirm trade. One way to determine the extent to which intrafirm trade is growing is to examine United States tariff items 806.30 and 807.00, which cover

### TABLE 10

**Leading African Exporters of Manufactures to Developed Market Economies ($ million)**

|             | 1962 | 1972 | 1975 |
|-------------|------|------|------|
| Zambia*     | 309  | 575  | 657  |
| Zaire*      | 213  | 430  | 542  |
| Ghana       | 32   | 110  | 216  |
| Ivory Coast | 8    | 87   | 178  |
| Nigeria     | 33   | 66   | 117  |
| Cameroon    | 28   | 48   | 77   |
| Kenya       | 16   | 32   | 55   |

*Primarily unworked nonferrous metals.

SOURCES: UNCTAD, *Review of Recent Trends and Developments in Trade in Manufactures and Semi-Manufactures*, TD/B/C.2/140, December 9, 1974, Table 15, p. 36; and *Recent Trends and Developments in Trade in Manufactures and Semi-Manufactures*, TD/B/C.2/175, May 11, 1977, Table 13, p. 24.

[50] Benjamin J. Cohen, *Multinational Firms and Asian Exports*, Yale University Press, New Haven, 1975, p. 10.

the tariff on the foreign value added of United States imports of items fabricated from United States components. United States imports from LDCs under these two tariff items increased from some $60.7 million in 1966 to $2245.9 million in 1975—an increase of over 3,000 percent.[51] Between 1966 and 1970, while total United States imports grew by 56.3 percent, imports by United States multinational firms from their own affiliates grew by 92.2 percent in the manufacturing sector and by 81.9 percent overall.[52]

Most of the large multinational corporations that have internationalized production are American, but increasingly firms from Britain, Germany, France, and some of the smaller countries of the EEC have shifted a share of their assets, production, and sales abroad. It is within the context of a competition among multinational firms for dominance in this changing international division of labor that one must evaluate the Lomé Convention between the EEC and 54 African, Caribbean, and Pacific (ACP) countries.

The Lomé Convention, it can be shown, is at one and the same time a means to preserve certain elements of the old international division of labor, with its extractive role for African political economies, and a device to encourage structural changes in both the European countries and selected African countries in keeping with the new distribution of manufacturing production. Its key provisions include measures to stabilize ACP export earnings from traditional products, measures to increase EEC direct investment in ACP countries, and measures to regulate access to the EEC market for ACP manufactures. The operation of these measures cannot be expected to deal effectively with the problems of growing inequalities, unemployment, and poverty of African ACP countries. These measures may instead be expected to create export-manufacturing enclaves and reinforce raw material producing enclaves, thereby maintaining the disarticulation of the ACP economies which generates these social problems.

[51]Michael Sharpston, "International Subcontracting," *World Development*, vol. 4, no. 4, April 1976, p. 33.

[52]Gerald K. Helleiner, "Freedom and Management in U.S. Primary Commodity Imports from Developing Countries," November 1976, p. 6. (Mimeographed)

This is clear from an analysis of the Stabex system—which is designed to stabilize ACP export earnings—and from a review of the relationship in Lomé between direct foreign investment and EEC manufactured goods access.

Stabex guarantees the relative stability of export earnings derived from the export of 11 traditional agricultural products and one mineral resource (iron ore). Unlike the common fund discussed at Nairobi during UNCTAD IV, Stabex does not try to stabilize the *price* of commodities but merely to compensate for shortfalls in export earnings due to price fluctuations. Only unprocessed commodities on the Stabex list qualify,[53] and only when export earnings fall below 7.5 percent of the average for the previous four years (2.5 percent for the more disadvantaged countries) can the country in question request a financial transfer. Even then such transfers can be denied when it is the opinion of the EEC that the decline in export earnings is caused by a trade policy that discriminates against the Community. A policy that directs commodities toward domestic processing and discourages the export of them in their raw state can be considered discriminatory.[54]

The Stabex system is, thus, both an incentive to maintain present levels of production in these specific commodities and a disincentive to diversify commercial agricultural production, process raw materials locally, or develop domestic food production—all activities that would promote domestic economic

[53]If an ACP country processes some of these commodities, thereby lowering its actual exports, it is ineligible to receive Stabex funds. As Hugh Ballam noted, Botswana's and Kenya's attempts to semiprocess some of their primary exports (beef and cut flowers, respectively) conflicted with the EEC's agricultural policy. "The STABEX and CAP combined make it less profitable to take the risks and costs of processing." These risks even extend to the loss of the EEC market. Hugh Ballam, "The Lomé Convention: Who Profits?," paper presented to the Council for European Studies/European Community Workshop on "The European Community and the Third World," Princeton, December 9–11, 1976, p. 7.

[54]Michael Dolan, "The Lomé Convention and Europe's Relations with the Third World: A Critical Analysis," paper prepared for presentation at the 18th Annual Meeting of the International Studies Association, St. Louis, March 16–20, 1977, p. 8.

linkages and bring the structures of demand and production more into line. Moreover, Stabex conforms to a growing need, expressed by EEC leaders, to guarantee sources of raw materials and energy resources—a position articulated with considerable force since the 1973 oil crisis. In using the Lomé Convention for this purpose, the EEC reconfirms the traditional role of the ACP states as the providers of primary products.

But EEC interests also lie in the furtherance of trade and direct foreign investment. While preserving one traditional Third World role, Lomé also facilitates the transformation of the domestic structures of industrial production in Third World countries in line with the needs of the multinational corporations. In this light, the linkage of direct foreign investment to trade through Title 1, Article 1 (which permits duty-free entry for ACP manufactures into the EEC), and Title III, Article 26 (which encourages direct foreign investment by EEC multinationals in the ACP), becomes clear. The EEC is anxious to guarantee preferential rights of establishment for EEC multinationals in ACP countries vis-à-vis their Japanese and American competitors. By agreeing to treat the ACP countries as a single customs territory, the EEC demonstrates that it is interested in facilitating the rationalization of the production of European multinationals throughout the ACP countries, thus making it possible for a French, German, or British multinational firm to maximize profits at the least cost by manufacturing components in different ACP countries, assembling them in still another ACP country, and then exporting the finished product back to the EEC duty-free. But the EEC through the Lomé Convention is equally anxious to prevent American and Japanese multinationals from engaging in the same process of rationalization within the ACP-EEC market, an objective that began with the EEC's general system of preferences (GSP).[55] To this end the lengthy rules of origin contained in the Lomé Convention are directed.

[55]"From the inception of the GSP of the EC, the United States called for the abolition of . . . preferences, whereby products could be imported under preferential rates if their processed materials had originated in the preference-giving country, according to the established GSP origin rules of the EC. This

The rules of origin deal specifically with the case of products not "wholly obtained" within the ACP and in the manufacture of which products coming from outside the EEC-ACP market are added. The final product will not be considered as originating in the ACP for the purpose of duty-free entry into the EEC market unless the components that originate in third countries are subject to sufficient working or processing—defined as incorporating a percentage of national value added which can range as high as 70 percent. Even then, as the rules of origin indicate, there are cases for which such working and processing may still not confer the status of "originating products."

While the EEC seeks to guarantee preferential rights of establishment for its multinationals vis-à-vis their Japanese or American rivals, the consequences of equality of treatment between large, EEC corporations and the smaller, nationally owned firms with which they must also compete (as stipulated in Title V, Article 62) imply effective discrimination against the latter in access to bank credit, skilled labor, tax incentives, and other benefits provided by the state. Title V, Chapter 2, of the Lomé Convention, moreover, contains a general prohibition against exchange controls or limits on the repatriation of profits, thereby inhibiting ACP governments from attempting to regulate direct foreign investment and technology transfer in the interest of domestic or regional development. Finally these provisions, given the above limitation on manufactured exports that contain non-EEC MNC components, narrow the field of foreign investors deemed desirable in the ACP, curtail the search for more appropriate technology suppliers than those found within the EEC, and thus reduce the bargaining power of ACP states in negotiations with EEC firms.

Although the growth of manufacturing industry in Third World countries and especially the growth of manufactured exports appears to many as a desirable objective, and its increase is taken

---

reduced the American export market for similar materials in the Third World." "Evolution of the Generalized System of Preferences of the European Communities: A Perspective," *Journal of World Trade Law*, vol. 10, no. 4, July/August 1976, p. 386.

as an indication that Third World countries are becoming "developed," this impression may be misleading. As with import-substituting industrialization, much depends upon the ownership structure of this new industry. To the extent that new export-oriented industry forms an integral part of an internationalized system of production, there is only the smallest probability that it will contribute to the promotion of greater congruence between the domestic structures of African demand and production, provide the internal dynamic for autonomous growth, or reduce the segmentation and disarticulation of African political economies. On the other hand, insofar as the EEC countries are concerned, there is every reason to expect that the Lomé Convention will strengthen the position of EEC multinationals in their competition with United States and Japanese firms. It is thus likely that the Lomé Convention will contribute to the emergence of an international division of labor that cannot but perpetuate the uneven development of the old.[56]

## EXPORT MANUFACTURING AND AFRICAN DEVELOPMENT

The implication of the previous section is not that increased export manufacturing in Africa cannot make a positive contribution to *development* as opposed to underdevelopment. It remains true that export manufacturing could (1) achieve much more buoyant export earnings for African countries than most primary production has done, (2) improve employment and income distribution prospects through the labor-intensive character of that manufacturing in which African countries have a "natural" comparative advantage internationally, (3) multiply internal economic linkages to the degree to which export manufacturing draws widely on internal raw material and intermediate input sources, and (4) improve manufacturing efficiency in

[56]Stephen Hymer, "The Multinational Corporation and the Law of Uneven Development," in Hugo Radice (ed.), *International Firms and Modern Imperialism*, Penguin Books, New York, 1976, pp. 37–62.

home markets because of the economies-of-scale approachable through export manufacturing.

The growth of such dynamic and positive export manufacturing, though, is not, we believe, likely to be encouraged by the internationalization strategies of MNCs. Such firms generally locate abroad only particular segments of an integrated production process. This means that domestic linkage effects will be very limited. A number of studies have found these restricted linkages to be the major distinguishing characteristic of MNC export subsidiaries in Taiwan and countries in Southeast Asia. Moreover, the "natural" expansion of exports from a given subsidiary is likely to run directly counter to the MNC preference to diversify its sourcing operations for a given input from one to a number of low-cost sources; both these points are documented in the Cohen study previously mentioned. Also, these segment-enterprises are unlikely to have any direct market in the Third World country itself, so that the lower consumer costs there that economies-of-scale might have generated (as above) simply are not a relevant concern. It may even be argued that the employment effects of multinational corporate export manufacturing may be limited, because the sorts of products they are manufacturing—even though it is the labor-intensive production segments of these products that are relocated—lend themselves to much more capital-intensive technology choices in *all* segments than is the case with traditional labor-intensive manufactures, such as shoes or textiles.

One condition of viable development being led by export manufacturing, then, may well be that domestic-owned enterprises organize this manufacturing. In that case, such manufacturing may be a natural outgrowth of the resource base of the African country—maximizing linkages, emphasizing employment of local labor, and also generating economy-of-scale efficiencies for local consumers. (One thinks, for instance, of Tanzania's exports of binder twine, based on local sisal inputs, and of textiles, based on local cotton, with domestic, labor-intensive state corporations in each case organizing this production.)

The longer-run feasibility of such labor-intensive, indigenous manufacturing exports remains very questionable, though. The basic labor-intensive products involved are bound to undercut some domestic production within, for instance, EEC countries. And such labor-intensive production within EEC countries is generally concentrated in poorer regions, in which the transfer opportunities for labor and capital are limited and in which structural factors often inhibit transfer to other regions.

In Europe the GATT Agreement caused a loss of about 400,000 jobs in the textile sector over a three-year period. This loss resulted in part from import competition and the higher cost of oil needed for synthetic fibers. The loss amounted to 10 percent of the workers in textiles, many of whom are women. Similar trends are also evident in shoes, leather, and clothing.[57] The loss of jobs due to the Agreement is now combined with the persistence of high levels of general unemployment, which would have been considered totally unacceptable a decade ago and which have imperiled the renegotiation of the Multifibre Agreement. This situation underlines the political economy realities of Third World manufacturing export expansion in this context. The European sectors hardest hit by transitions such as the growth of textile imports are often regionally concentrated and resist the change. This resistance is legitimate if the group is being forced to bear the full burden of the transition. The key question then becomes, "By what *political* and *economic* mechanisms can the costs of change be socialized and the change be made more acceptable to immediately affected parties?"[58]

It must be recognized that an effective answer to this industrial adjustment policy question is a prerequisite for dramatic expansion of developmental export manufacturing in African countries. And such an answer almost certainly requires much more buoyant economic conditions in the industrialized countries to be effective. In the absence of such conditions, trade barriers are increasingly established by industrialized countries against such Third World imports (as with the recent French imposition of import quotas on textile products).

[57]Brian Van Arkadie and C. Logan, "The Economic and Political Context and Research Priorities," in *Conference on Adjustment Policy*, Institute of Social Studies, The Hague, 1977, p. 36.
[58]Ibid., p. 30.

It is, however, important to note that such import restrictions are generally applied selectively, allowing continued Third World exports in particular product areas where strong political forces in the center countries have an interest in defending trade access. *This* is almost certainly the critical basis of the diversified access of Third World manufactured goods into the United States economy, an access that has been evident across many more industries than the pattern for OECD countries as a whole.[59] Assuming that the same forces are at work in the political economy of trade restriction in the EEC countries, this dynamic builds in a powerful advantage for European multinational firms in organizing the trade expansion associated with the new African-European relations. Moreover, so long as European multinationals can organize the relocation of production that *they* wish to, they are unlikely to press for the establishment of more comprehensive industrial adjustment instruments that would allow a wider and less selective trade access to EEC countries.

There appear, then, to be two broad alternative patterns by which African export manufacturing for European markets could expand: (1) a combination of domestically developed export of simpler manufactured goods, based on local inputs, with an activist industrial adjustment policy in Europe to socialize transition costs in manufacturing there; or (2) a combination of MNC relocation of segments of their manufacturing process within enclaves in Africa, coupled with selective trade restrictions in Europe that mesh with these MNC strategies.

While the first alternative would appear to be far and away the most beneficial for African development, it appears to us that the second alternative is more likely to be the actual pattern of events.

The reasons for this may be summarized briefly. First, macroeconomic employment conditions in the Western capitalist economies generally do not appear likely to improve much in the next five years, making it very difficult to expect effective industrial adjustment strategies to emerge in Europe. Second,

[59]Helleiner, "Transnational Enterprises and the New Political Economy of U.S. Trade Policy," *Oxford Economic Papers*, vol. 29, no. 1, March 1977.

where such strategies have been formulated—as in the Netherlands and Sweden—small, well-integrated economies have been involved and the relevant governments have been quite interventionist and prepared to confront dominant local corporations with a counterlogic of social investment planning or state enterprise. These conditions do not characterize the great range of industrialized countries. Both of these realities suggest that trade restrictions in the so-called First World will increase in the medium-term future.

A third reason derives from the political-economic realities of many African countries, as noted earlier. There is often a close symbiosis between the dominant local classes of such countries and multinational enterprise, meaning that local policy is very unlikely to restrict multinational export manufacturing and to try to organize domestic alternatives to it. Thus the *first* condition for viable development is unlikely to be met either.

Export manufacturing in Africa, then, will undoubtedly increase—as the signs of change in such countries as the Ivory Coast, Senegal, Ghana, and Kenya suggest. But this manufacturing is likely to be largely under the direction of foreign enterprises and integrated into the structure of internationalized production. In consequence, the linkage, employment, and income effects of such manufacturing will be fairly limited within Africa—and probably will be enjoyed mainly by those local elites who will extend their import-substitution symbiosis to the export sector. Significant restructuring of African economies, with wide dynamic advantages for African majorities, cannot be expected to emerge from this export-manufacturing growth.

## A NEW INTERNATIONAL ECONOMIC ORDER AND AFRICA?

So far this discussion of emerging options has focused on African-European relations. But the possibilities of restructuring the international economy have been discussed in a wider context than that. A full-scale program for restructuring has been articulated by Third World countries and explored in some detail in a number of analyses. To what extent might such extensive international restructuring take place, and what is the likelihood that it would generate development in Africa?

On the first question, Van Arkadie and Logan supply a careful and realistic appraisal—with a very pessimistic conclusion. We can do no better than to quote from their analysis:

Is the appeal to a combination of the loftier sentiments, and to a general and longer term well-being of all, sufficient to provide an impetus to make proposals for such significant negotiated changes practical in the face of the history of UNCTAD's failures and in the light of the particular short-term pressures that national governments now face?

The sad fact is that even if such proposals are eminently practical in that their implementation would provide widespread economic improvements in both developed and developing countries and a much more desirable outcome than many other scenarios, it does not mean that there is a practical sequence of negotiation possibilities which will readily arise out of the existing political and economic situations in which governments find themselves. . . .Policies aimed at restructuring the world economy to the mutual benefit of North and South do not appear to be emerging from the industrialized world in response to the demands and aspirations of the Third World.[60]

Only at the level of changes in world commodity markets does some restructuring seem a possibility, with a common fund for stabilization now having been accepted in principle (though divisions on implementation remain strong) and with agreements having been negotiated for certain of the core commodities on the UNCTAD list of raw materials. When the Ministerial Meetings of the North-South Conference ended in June 1977, however, the "South" chairman, Mr. Perez-Guerrero of Venezuela, concluded that no substantive concessions had been made in response to the basic needs of the Third World; in particular, there had been no progress toward protecting their purchasing power or improving their access to the First World's markets and technology.

[60]Van Arkadie and Logan, "The Economic and Political Context," pp. 30, 39–40.

The chances of extensive change, then, appear very limited. Moreover, the significance of potential international-level changes needs to be critically examined in the African context. International efforts are vital to the development process, but they are no substitute for commitment within LDCs toward appropriate policies and reforms that benefit the poorest citizens. Particularly in African countries, the fact that the great majority of people remain within a peasant mode of production suggests that internal policy measures will be crucial to the improvement of people's lives. Although commodity-price stabilizations (or, indeed, increases) can obviously contribute to such improvement, there is no guarantee that they will do so in the context of many of the domestic economic growth strategies that characterize African countries. Such stabilization or increases may simply allow faster import-substituting industrialization, with multinational firms and their African partners or managers capturing the bulk of benefits; or they may accelerate multinational-organized export manufacturing, with few spread effects locally and concentrated advantages (again) going to the local elites; or the improved earnings may simply be used for more imports of arms and luxury goods, reinforcing state repression and strengthening the resistance to change of local African bourgeoisies.

The debate over a new international economic order, then, is also unlikely to result in fundamental change in the patterns of African underdevelopment discussed in this paper.

# FIVE

# Conclusion

At one level, the conclusions of this paper are bleak. Historical analysis of precolonial and colonial Africa shows how the economic and social structuring of these periods built in wide inequalities, considerable poverty, and serious constraints on change throughout the continent. The symbiosis of MNCs with African petit bourgeois forces that existed after independence blocked developmental responses to these realities—with the industrialization that occurred working mainly to the advantage of small minorities and with the benefits of regional integration being enjoyed mostly by wealthier states. Preliminary analysis suggests that similar forces will distort the distribution of any potential gains from the changing international division of labor that is evident in European-African relations.

At this level, the historical and continuing strength of dependency ties is discouraging. At another level, however, a more promising conclusion may be possible. The contradictions of underdevelopment in many African countries are clearly evident in our discussion above. And these realities are as clearly pushing some countries to alternative approaches. In such nations as Tanzania, Mozambique, Guinea-Bissau, Angola, and Sao Tomé, regimes are devising "self-reliance" strategies designed to escape the worst effects of dependency and to build development rather than underdevelopment. Just as the constraints of colonialism ultimately were challenged and rejected through political struggles, so we expect many other African countries to be

pushed, by domestic political forces in the 1980s, to similar reactions against the constraints of periphery capitalism. Not all
African countries will move in that direction; those few privileged
nations that are deeply incorporated into the international capitalist economy—such as the Ivory Coast or Kenya—may find
the symbiosis between local and foreign capital powerful enough
to resist radical change. But for most African countries, the
incapacity of the present international capitalist system to adjust
sufficiently to draw most Third World people much more com-
prehensively into the international division of labor can be expected to force such peoples to adopt more imaginative and
creative strategies, with unhappy human costs of transition but
long-run developmental advantages.

What directions might self-reliant development strategies best
take in Africa?

The essential priority of such alternative strategies has been
captured by the International Labor Organization (ILO)'s notion
of emphasizing the satisfaction of basic human needs. These are
defined as the minimum living standards that a society should
set for its poorest people. Each family's minimum requirements
for food, shelter, clothing, safe drinking water, sanitation, transport, health, and education must be met. In addition, each person
available for and willing to work should have an adequately
remunerated job. Basic needs also imply a healthy, humane, and
satisfying environment; popular participation in decisions affecting the lives and livelihood of the people; and individual
freedom.[61]

At the heart of a basic needs strategy and essential to greater
self-reliance is a successful agricultural policy that permits the
vast majority of Africans to achieve adequate food production
on land over which they have control and assure that these
majorities will participate fully in productivity and income gains
throughout the whole rural sector. This policy involves rejection
of a "bimodal" agricultural development pattern, in which a
small "modern" sector of larger farms is encouraged to advance
while most peasants stagnate, and endorsement instead of a

[61]International Labor Organization, *Employment, Growth and Basic Needs:
A One World Problem*, ILO, Geneva, 1976, p. 7.

"unimodal" or frontal rural strategy in which all share.[62] Such frontal patterns require, inter alia, equitable land distribution, widely distributive credit and marketing policies, and intense attention to the creation of rural institutions that can proliferate new information, collectivize the risks that otherwise inhibit innovation among small peasants, and give local peasants enough political strength to enforce equitable sharing of agricultural gains.[63]

While domestic food production is the first priority for self-reliance, this does not mean that much of Africa cannot support some nonfood agricultural production. Increasingly, however, this production should be integrated with local industrial production, in order to help build up a dynamic, autonomous, and more interlinked domestic economy. More convergence between local consumption needs and the local production base is central to a strategy of self-reliance.[64] Such a convergence strategy can be expected to generate much more local production of basic consumer goods, building material, and even capital equipment—using more labor-intensive techniques and local inputs and thereby increasing employment and linkage effects from industrialization.

Considerable income redistribution and marked efforts against the dominance of multinational enterprises are crucial to such shifts. Only through such changes can the consumer-demand patterns of African countries be restructured to mesh with the labor-intensive, local-linkage-intensive output implied by the convergence strategy. Such a revamped industrial policy, too, should emphasize small-scale and rural industrialization if wide income effects are to be obtained.[65]

[62]Bruce F. Johnston and Peter Kilby, *Agriculture and Structural Transformation: Economic Strategies in Late-Developing Countries*, Oxford University Press, New York, 1975.

[63]John Weeks, "Uncertainty, Risk and Wealth and Income Distribution in Peasant Agriculture," *Journal of Development Studies*, October 1970.

[64]Havelock Brewster and Clive Thomas, "Aspects of the Theory of Economic Integration," *Journal of Common Market Studies*, December 1969, pp. 110–132.

[65]See D. Vail, *Technology for Ujamaa Village Development in Tanzania*, Maxwell School of Citizenship and Public Affairs, Syracuse University, Syracuse, 1975, on Tanzanian efforts in this direction.

Essential for success in all these respects is increased technological self-reliance. A broadly based agricultural strategy requires diffusion of technological improvements relevant to small-scale peasants rather than the capital-intensive emphasis of agricultural innovation in the North; and a decentralized, linkage-intensive industrial policy also requires technological innovation in much different directions than that promoted by multinational firms. Such developments of "appropriate technology" will come only from efforts made within the less developed countries—efforts that are connected much more effectively to the indigenous structure of production than has often been true of scientific and technological efforts in the Third World. Such technological self-reliance, of course, does not imply autarky in knowledge production for the Third World. But it does imply (1) much more capacity to scan the world widely for such knowledge, (2) much greater ability to manage and ease technology transfers that are essential, and (3) much more capacity to generate indigenous technological knowledge appropriate to a given local environment.

There are various reforms in the international political economy that could contribute to such broad strategies of self-reliant development. Measures to liberalize the context of international technology transfer, for instance, would make it easier for poor African countries to avoid extensive dependence on multinational firms; among key reforms to this end would be the restructuring of the international patent system (to allow Third World countries to discriminate in their own favor and to establish stricter regulations on developed-country patent holders to allow licensing at reasonable prices in the Third World). Creation of a code of conduct for technology transfer could also help— and so would international funding for regional Third World technology centers. Even more significant could be trade policy developments in the world economy. Forms of export-price stabilization, as through the UNCTAD Common Fund proposals, could make some contribution to self-reliance strategies by reducing the large fluctuations that disrupt indigenous planning efforts. More important, however, could be development of South-South trade links, gradually eclipsing present North-South patterns; and institutional reforms, such as the establishment of a currency to be used only for such trade,[66] could assist such change. More South-South trade could allow African countries to capture industrial economies-of-scale through exports without having to adopt the often inappropriate technology required to produce for Western capitalist markets.

Such South-South trade in the African context could be especially useful on a continental basis. But the prospect of such development depends heavily on successful overthrow of the white-run regimes in Southern Africa. The possibility of that taking place is likely to be a central focus of much international concern in Africa, on many levels, throughout the 1980s. Self-reliant black regimes in Namibia, Zimbabwe, and South Africa would make an immense contribution to alternative development strategy for all Africa, but considerable conflict will occur before such regimes finally emerge.

Armed conflict in Southern Africa, though, is likely to be no more than the most dramatic African form of confrontation between dependence and self-reliance in the 1980s. We expect the contradictions of periphery capitalism in Africa to become more acute in most countries on the continent in the next decade, and we expect the struggles for change in such countries to become more bitter as a result. We are confident, however, that out of such conflict can come more equitable and self-reliant development strategies that benefit the great majority of Africans.

<hr/>

[66]Frances Stewart, "The Direction of International Trade: Gains and Losses for the Third World," in G. K. Helleiner (ed.), *A World Divided: The Less Developed Countries in the International Economy*, Cambridge University Press, London, 1976, pp. 89–112.

# Selected Bibliography

Adam, Heribet (ed.): *South Africa: Sociological Perspectives*, Oxford University Press, New York, 1971.

Adelman, Irma, and Cynthia Taft Morris: *Economic Growth and Social Equity in Developing Countries*, Stanford University Press, Stanford, Calif., 1973.

Ake, Claude: "Explanatory Notes on the Political Economy of Africa," *Journal of Modern African Studies*, vol. 14, no. 1, 1976, pp. 1–23.

Amin, Samir: "Underdevelopment and Dependence," *Journal of Modern African Studies*, vol. 10, no. 4, December 1972, pp. 503–525.

Anise, Ladun: "Trends in Leadership Succession and Regime Change in African Politics since Independence," *African Studies Review*, vol. 17, no. 3, 1974, pp. 5–524.

Balandier, Georges: *Ambiguous Africa: Cultures in Collision*, London, Chatto and Windus, London, 1966.

Brett, E. A.: *Colonialism and Underdevelopment in East Africa: The Politics of Economic Change 1919–1939*, Nok, New York, 1973.

Campbell, B.: "Social Change and Class Formation in a French West African State," *Canadian Journal of African Studies*, vol. 8, no. 2, 1974.

Carr, E. H.: *Nationalism and After*, Macmillan, London, 1945.

Carter, Gwen: *Politics of Inequality: South Africa since 1948*, Thames and Hudson, London, 1958.

Cervenka, Zdenek: *The Unfinished Quest for Unity: Africa and the OAU*, Friedmann, London, 1977.

Chancellor, W. J., and J. R. Goss: "Balancing Energy and Food Production, 1975–2000," *Science*, vol. 192, no. 4236, 1976, pp. 213–218.

Chenery, Hollis, et al.: *Redistribution with Growth*, Oxford University Press, New York, 1974.

Cohen, Michael: "Cities in Developing Countries: 1975–2000," *Finance and Development*, vol. 13, no. 1, 1976, pp. 12–15.

Cruise O'Brien, Rita: "Factors of Dependence: Senegal and Kenya," Anglo-French Colloquium on Independence and Dependence, Paris, 1976.

Davidson, Basil: *The African Past*, Longmans, London, 1964.

De Klerk, William A.: *Puritans in Africa: A Study of the Afrikaners*, Collins, London, 1977.

Díaz-Alejandro, Carlos F.: "North-South Relations: The Economic Component," *International Organization*, vol. 29, Winter 1975, pp. 213–241.

Dos Santos, T.: "The Crisis of Development Theory and the Problem of Dependence in Latin America," in H. Bernstein (ed.), *Underdevelopment and Development*, Penguin, New York, 1973, pp. 57–80.

Elliott, Charles: *Patterns of Poverty in the Third World*, Praeger, New York, 1975.

Freeman, C.: *The Economics of Industrial Innovation*, Penguin, New York, 1974.

Furtado, Celso: *Development and Underdevelopment*, University of California Press, Berkeley, 1967.

Geiss, Imanuel: *The Pan-African Movement*, Methuen, London, 1974.

Gray, Richard, and David Birmingham: "Some Economic and Political Consequences of Trade in Central and Eastern Africa in the Pre-Colonial Period," in Richard Gray and David Birmingham (eds.), *Pre-Colonial African Trade*, Oxford University Press, New York, 1970, pp. 1–24.

Helleiner, Gerald K.: "International Technology Issues: Southern Needs and Northern Responses," in Jagdish N. Bhagwati, *The New International Economic Order: The North-South Debate*, MIT Press, Boston, 1977.

———: "Transnational Enterprises and the New Political Economy of U.S. Trade Policy," *Oxford Economic Papers*, vol. 29, no. 1, March 1977, pp. 102–116.

Hill, P.: *Migrant Cocoa-Farmers of Southern Ghana: A Study in Rural Capitalism*, Cambridge University Press, New York, 1963.

Hopkins, Anthony G.: *An Economic History of West Africa*, Columbia University Press, New York, 1973.

Hopkins, Raymond: *Political Roles in a New State: Tanzania's First Decade*, Yale University Press, New Haven, 1971.

Hymer, Stephen: "The Multinational Corporation and the Law of Uneven Development," in H. Radice (ed.), *International Firms and Modern Imperialism*, Penguin, New York, 1975, pp. 37–62.

International Labor Organization: *Employment, Growth and Basic Needs: A One World Problem*, ILO, Geneva, 1976.

——: *Employment, Incomes and Equality*, ILO, Geneva, 1972.

Johnson, R. W.: *How Long Will South Africa Survive?* Macmillan, London, 1977.

July, Robert W.: *The Origins of Modern African Thought*, Faber, London, 1968.

Kedourie, Elie (ed.): *Nationalism in Asia and Africa*, Weidenfeld, London, 1971.

Kilby, Peter: *Industrialization in an Open Economy: Nigeria, 1945–66*, Cambridge University Press, New York, 1969.

Killick, Tony: "The Benefits of Foreign Direct Investment and Its Alternatives: An Empirical Exploration," *Journal of Development Studies*, vol. 9, no. 2, 1973, pp. 301–316.

Kitchen, Helen (ed.): *Africa: From Mystery to Maze,* Lexington Books, Lexington, Mass., 1977.

Kohn, Hans: *The Idea of Nationalism*, Macmillan, New York, 1946.

Langdon, Steven: "Multinational Corporations. Taste Transfer and Underdevelopment: A Case Study from Kenya," *Review of African Political Economy*, vol. 1, no. 2, 1975, pp. 12–35.

——: "Technology Transfer by Multinational Corporations in Africa: Effects on the Economy," *African Development*, vol. 2, no. 2, 1977, pp. 95–114.

Legum, Colin: *Pan-Africanism: A Brief History*, Greenwood Press, New York, 1964.

——: *The Year of the Whirlwind*, Africana, New York, 1977.

——: *The West's Crisis in Southern Africa*, Africana, New York, 1978.

——, and Tony Hodges: *After Angola: A Study of International Involvement*, Africana, New York, 1976.

——, and W. Lee: *Conflict in the Horn of Africa*, Africana, New York, 1977.

LeVine, Victor: *Political Leadership in Africa*, Hoover Institution, Stanford, Calif., 1967.

————: "Problems of Political Succession in Independent Africa," in Ali Mazrui and Hasu Patel (eds.), *Africa in World Affairs*, The Third Press, New York, 1973.

————: "Leadership Transition in Black Africa," paper presented to the African Studies Association, 1973.

Leys, Colin: *Underdevelopment in Kenya*, University of California Press, Berkeley, 1975.

Linneman, H., et al.: *Food for a Growing World Population*, Free University Economic and Social Institute, Amsterdam, 1976.

Miles, C.: "Adjustment Assistance Policies: A Survey," in *Adjustment for Trade: Studies on Individual Adjustment Problems and Policies*, OECD Development Centre, Paris, 1975.

Murray, Roger: "Second Thoughts on Ghana," *New Left Review*, vol. 42, 1967.

Mutiso, Godfrey C. M.: "Cleavage and the Organizational Base of Politics in Kenya: A Theoretical Framework," *Journal of Eastern African Research and Development*, vol. 3, no. 1, 1973.

Mytelka, Lynn: "A Genealogy of Francophone West and Equatorial African Regional Organisations," *Journal of Modern African Studies*, vol. 12, no. 2, 1974, pp. 297–320.

————: "The Lomé Convention and a New International Division of Labour," *Journal of European Integration*, vol. 1, no. 1, 1977, pp. 63–73.

Nyerere, Julius K.: *Freedom and Development*, Oxford University Press, New York, 1974.

Öberdörfer, Dieter: "Schwarz-Afrika im Jahr 2000," in D. Öberdörfer (ed.), *Africana Collecta*, Bertelsmann, Freiburg, 1968.

Oliver, Roland, and J. G. Fage: *A Short History of Africa*, Penguin, London, 1962.

Potholm, Christian P.: "Toward the Millennium," in C. Potholm and Richard Dale (eds.), *Southern Africa in Perspective*, Free Press, New York, 1972.

Ranger, T. O. (ed.): *Emerging Themes of African History*, Heinemann, London, 1968.

Rathbone, R.: "Businessmen in Politics: Party Struggle in Ghana, 1949–57," *Journal of Development Studies*, vol. 9, no. 3, 1973, pp. 391–401.

Sagasti, F. R.: "Technological Self-Reliance and Co-operation among Third World Countries," *World Development*, vol. 4, 1976, pp. 939–946.

Schneider, William: *Food, Foreign Policy and Raw Materials Cartels*, Crane, Russak, New York, 1976.

Servoise, René: "Whither Black Africa?" in Bertrand de Jouvenal (ed.), *Futuribles I*, Droz, Geneva, 1963.

Shaw, Timothy: "The International Politics of Southern Africa: Change or Continuity?" paper presented to the African Studies Association, 1976.

———: "Dependence or Development: International or Internal Inequalities in Africa," paper presented to the African Studies Association, 1976.

Shivji, I.: *Class Struggles in Tanzania*, Monthly Review, New York, 1976.

Spence, J. E.: *The Political and Military Framework of External Investment in South Africa*, Africa Publications Trust, London, 1975.

Stewart, Frances: *Technology and Underdevelopment*, Macmillan, London, 1977.

Suckling, John, et al.: *The Economic Factor of External Investment in South Africa*, Africa Publications Trust, London, 1975.

Sunkel, Osvaldo: "Transnational Capitalism and National Disintegration in Latin America," *Social and Economic Studies*, vol. 22, no. 1, March 1973, pp. 132–176.

Teriba, O., E. C. Edozien, and M. O. Kayode: "Some Aspects of Ownership and Control Structure of Business Enterprise in a Developing Economy: The Nigerian Case," *Nigerian Journal of Economic and Social Studies*, vol. 14, no. 1, 1972, pp. 3–25.

Thomas, W. H., et al.: *The Conditions of the Black Worker in South Africa*, African Publications Trust, London, 1975.

Thompson, Leonard, and Jeffrey Butler (eds.): *Change in Contemporary South Africa*, University of California Press, Berkeley, 1975.

Trezise, Philip H., and C. Fred Bergsten: "After Oil, Bananas and Bauxite?" *Brookings Bulletin*, vol. 11, no. 2, 1974, pp. 6–10.

Touval, Saadia: *The Boundary Politics of Independent Africa*, Harvard University Press, Boston, 1972.

UNCTAD: *Recent Trends and Developments in Trade in Manufactures and Semi-Manufactures*, TD/B/C.2/175, May 11, 1977.

Wallerstein, Immanuel: *Africa: The Politics of Independence*, Knopf, New York, 1961.

Weeks, John: "The Problem of Wage Policy in Developing Countries with Special Reference to Africa," *The Economic Bulletin of Ghana*, vol. 1, no. 1, 2nd series, 1971.

Weil, Herman, and John McIlroy: *Stochastic Simulations of Long-Range Forecasting Models*, CACI, Inc., Arlington, Va., 1975.

Zartman, I. William: "Europe and Africa: Decolonization or Dependency?" *Foreign Affairs*, vol. 54, no. 2, 1976, pp. 325–343.

——: "The Circulation of Elites," in I. William Zartman (ed.), *The Study of Middle East Elites*, Princeton University Press, Princeton, 1978.

——: "The Policy Challenges," in Jennifer S. Whitaker (ed.), *United States and Africa*, New York University Press, New York, forthcoming.

# Index

# About the Authors

COLIN LEGUM, an associate editor and Commonwealth correspondent of *The Observer* (London), writes frequently on Africa. His interests also include other Third World areas, as well as the Middle East. Mr. Legum was born in South Africa in 1919, where he began a journalistic and political career at the age of 16. Since joining *The Observer* in 1949, he has specialized in analysis of the Third World and, in particular, African independence movements. Mr. Legum is the author of numerous books, for example, the annual *Africa Contemporary Record; Pan-Africanism; After Angola: The War over Southern Africa; Vorster's Gamble in Africa;* and *Still Only the Whirlwind*. His most recent books are *The West's Crisis in Southern Africa* and, with William Lee, *Reshaping the Horn of Africa*.

I. WILLIAM ZARTMAN is a professor and the former head of the politics department at New York University. He has authored or contributed to several books, among them *International Relations in the New Africa; The Politics of Trade Negotiations Between Africa and the European Economic Community; Man, State and Society in the Contemporary Maghreb* (editor and co-author); *African Diplomacy;* and *Africa and the United States: Vital Interests*. Professor Zartman has received research grants from the Rockefeller and National Science foundations and a Fulbright-Hayes grant, among others. He has an M.A. from Johns Hopkins and a Ph.D. from Yale and is a member of the Council on Foreign Relations.

231

STEVEN LANGDON received a B.A. in economics and political science from the University of Toronto, an M.A. in Canadian studies from Carleton University, and a Ph.D. from Sussex University in England. Currently he is an assistant professor at Carleton University in Ottawa. Professor Langdon is particularly interested in international economic development, multinational corporations, and African affairs, and he has written several articles and studies on these subjects.

LYNN K. MYTELKA is an associate professor of political science at Carleton University in Ottawa. She has also worked as a research associate at the Institut de Coopération Internationale de l'Université d'Ottawa and at the Center for International Affairs, Harvard University. Professor Mytelka received her B.A. from Douglass College, Rutgers University, and her M.A. and Ph.D. from Johns Hopkins University. International relations, the political economy of development (Africa and Latin America), and comparative politics are her fields of interest. She is the author of numerous articles dealing with these subjects.

CATHERINE GWIN is a Project Fellow and the Executive Director of the 1980s Project of the Council on Foreign Relations.

## DATE DUE

| | | | |
|---|---|---|---|
| AP 29'80 | | | |
| FE 10'81 | | | |
| FE 23'81 | | | |
| MB 9'81 | | | |
| MR 26'81 | | | |
| AG 7'81 | | | |
| AG 11'81 | | | |
| OC 22'81 | | | |
| NO 4 '81 | | | |
| NO 30'81 | | | |
| DE 14'81 | | | |
| MR 18'82 | | | |
| AP 21'82 | | | |
| MR 12'84 | | | |
| AG 3 '84 | | | |
| AP 24'85 | | | |
| APR 2 '87 | | | |
| GAYLORD | | | PRINTED IN U.S.A |